Praise for Dr. Ishikawa's Work

"In 1981, Ford Motor Company began a very intense effort to improve product quality to achieve "Best-in-Class" levels in all world automotive markets. We knew that results would not be immediate since a change of this magnitude requires long range planning, vastly different operational disciplines, and ongoing training for all company employees.

We also know that quality improvement must be continuous without regard to short-term objectives and goals.

Our first involvement with the Japanese Union of Scientists and Engineers (JUSE) was in March 1982 when Ford sponsored a statistical study mission to Japan. This began a long and fruitful relationship with Dr. Ishikawa which continues today. In 1983, Dr. Ishikawa was kind enough to visit Ford on several occasions and conduct top-management training seminars for senior Ford executives, including myself, and in various positions including general management, product engineering, manufacturing, and marketing.

Our experiences with Dr. Ishikawa have helped us develop a whole new approach to quality which is embodied in the Japanese philosophy and operational aspects of "Company-wide Quality Control" (CWQC). Ford Motor Company is deeply indebted to Dr. Ishikawa for his contribution to our efforts. We look forward to a lasting association with the Japanese Union of Scientists and Engineers as we work toward achieving our goal of producing the highest quality cars and trucks in the world."

H. A. Poling, President
Chief Operating Officer
Ford Motor Company

"In 1962, when Bridgestone was preparing to institute a TQC program, it sought Dr. Kaoru Ishikawa to be its consultant. It was one of the best moves we ever made. As we went through our plan of TQC introduction, we experienced the joy of being guided by the very man who was responsible for developing TQC in Japan.

Two years later as President of Bridgestone, I announced the introduction of TQC. I went through Dr. Ishikawa's many books, reading them over and over again. I can recall fondly how Dr. Ishikawa taught us to organize and manage our QC circles, conscious of the fact that the founding father of the TQC movement was in our midst.

The practice of TQC is no longer confined to Japanese companies, and it is fast becoming a worldwide movement. *What Is Total Quality Control? The Japanese Way* is the distillation of over 30 years of experience, acquired by Dr. Ishikawa in giving guidance to countless TQC programs. It is most appropriate that it is being translated into English and published by Prentice-Hall.

I fervently hope that the book will be utilized not only in the United States but in the rest of the world."

Kanichiro Ishibashi
Chairman and CEO
Bridgestone Co., Ltd.

"TQC was introduced to Komatsu in 1961 to prepare us for the drastically changing business climate caused by the new waves of trade and capital liberalization. Since that time Dr. Ishikawa has been our effective mentor. He taught us a great deal. My company, my employees, and I are deeply indebted to him.

Komatsu has attained its present prominence in no small measure to its application of TQC. From TQC's early introduction in Japan until today, Dr. Ishikawa has tirelessly devoted his energy to its dissemination. It is no wonder that there are many overseas concerns along with Japanese companies who continue to seek his guidance.

Dr. Ishikawa's book is a storehouse of knowledge about TQC in which the essence of TQC is neatly summarized and explained in an easy to understand fashion. It tells its readers how to institute and promote TQC step by step. I have practiced TQC for many years, and I know it well. Yet, even I am constantly amazed by how much more I can still learn from this book."

Ryoichi Kawai
Chairman and CEO
Komatsu Manufacturing, Ltd.

"David Lu's translation is likely to be regarded as a lasting contribution to the industrialized world and to those nations seeking an industrial future. Japanese Total Quality Control provides sound guidance for managers who believe in achieving the highest possible standards of quality throughout their organizations."

Takeo Shiina
Chief Executive Officer
IBM Japan, Ltd.

"At Cummins, we have tried to understand the ways in which total quality assurance programs have been implemented and practiced in Japanese industries. We have explored the sources of preventive quality concepts in the works of W. E. Deming, V. Feigenbaum, and J. M. Juran, and we have tried to learn more about implementation by developing our contacts with Japanese firms that successfully practice total quality control. Furthermore, we have drawn on the skills and knowledge of current practitioners and teachers of comprehensive approaches to quality.

Dr. Ishikawa has been one of the most prominent and helpful individual resources on which we have drawn in developing our capability to increase the effectiveness of our quality assurance programs. As a consultant, he has a broad and deep understanding of total quality control both in the abstract and in practice. Furthermore, he is an exceptionally able teacher, advocate, and communicator.

I look forward to reading the translation of his *What Is Total Quality Control? The Japanese Way*. It will undoubtedly be an important addition to the literature on approaches to quality assurance, and, therefore, will benefit manufacturing firms in the U.S. and around the world as they strive to bring their quality to competitive levels."

James A. Henderson
President & Chief Operating Officer
Cummins Engine Company, Inc.

"Dr. Ishikawa has the ability to take a complex subject, break it down into its elements, and present it in a very readable and understandable manner. This talent and his in-depth knowledge of production and the service industries make this book a very valuable addition to any manager's or quality professional's library. The American Society for Quality Control appreciates his work and the close personal and professional relationship that we have."

John L. Hansel
President
American Society for Quality Control

What Is Total
Quality Control?
The Japanese Way

What Is Total Quality Control?
The Japanese Way

by

Kaoru Ishikawa

Translated by David J. Lu

Originally Titled: *TQC towa Nanika—
Nipponteki Hinshitsu Kanri (What Is Quality
Control? The Japanese Way)*

PRENTICE-HALL, INC.
Englewood Cliffs, N.J.

Prentice-Hall International, Inc. *London*
Prentice-Hall of Australia, Pty. Ltd., *Sydney*
Prentice-Hall Canada Inc., *Toronto*
Prentice-Hall of India Private Ltd., *New Delhi*
Prentice-Hall of Japan, Inc., *Tokyo*
Prentice-Hall of Southeast Asia Pte. Ltd., *Singapore*
Whitehall Books, Ltd, *Wellington, New Zealand*
Editora Prentice-Hall do Brasil, Ltda., *Rio de Janeiro*
Prentice-Hall Hispanoamericana, S.A., *Mexico*

© 1985 by
David J. Lu

20 19 18 17 16 15 14 13 12 11
10 9 8 7 6 5   PBK

Originally printed in Japan as
*TQC towa Nanika—Nipponteki
Hinshitsu Kanri (What Is Quality
Control? The Japanese Way)* by Ka-
oru Ishikawa. © Kaoru Ishikawa
1984, 1981, published by JUSE
Press. English language edition
arranged through Japan Foreign-
Rights Centre.

Library of Congress Cataloging in Publication Data

Ishikawa, Kaoru,
  What is total quality control?

  Includes index.
  1. Quality control—Japan. I. Title.
II. Title: Japanese way.
TS156.I8313 1985   658.5′62   84-26265
ISBN 0-13-952433-9
ISBN 0-13-952441-X   PBK

Printed in the United States of America

Translator's Introduction

A number of years ago when I was sitting across the table from an executive of CBS/Sony, discussing the state of the economy in Japan, the executive stated, almost casually, "Lately we have been having a number of visitors from the United States and Europe who want to observe our latest technology in phonograph record making. They know that our records sound better, but once they step inside our factory they discover that we use the same technology, the same pressing machine, and the same raw materials. Some visitors insist that we are using secret solutions and want to inspect our residue. Of course they do not find anything that is different from what they find in residues at home. They look puzzled when I tell them that the difference in the quality of sound comes from our people and not from our machines."

In making this statement, the executive of this United States-Japan joint venture company has provided one of the best explanations for the strength of Japanese economy. Of course we cannot discount the huge investment Japan has made in plants and equipment that has given Japan its relative strength in recent years. But machines can be duplicated elsewhere. On the other hand, if we were to remove those dedicated workers from their workplaces, Japanese industry would suddenly and surely find itself losing its luster.

There are many ways of looking at Japan's postwar economic miracles, but in the final analysis, human factors must come to the fore. Japanese management has somehow found the secret of harnessing the energy of its people more effectively than anyone else. This has been accomplished in large measure by a device called quality control (QC).

It is certainly impressive to observe the control room of Nippon Kokan K. K.'s Ohgishima plant, which represents the latest in steel making technology in the world. It is even more impressive, however, to see the plant's workers assemble in small quality circles. They share their expertise, discuss the problems they have encountered, and help one another in finding solutions.

The atmosphere is calm and the proceedings are orderly but the intent is serious. Through these meetings workers communicate freely with their foremen and engineers. At times, suggestions made by line workers are accepted ahead of those of engineers. There is a collegial feeling, and the meeting becomes a place for mutual development. The control room functions well precisely because its workers are educated, trained, and supported by quality circles. This practice is followed everywhere, from giants like Toyota to some of the small venture capital companies. It is also adopted by United States companies like IBM Japan. In fact, one of the marks of an excellent company in Japan is that it has a good total quality control (TQC) program.

The present volume is a full translation of a basic book on quality control by Dr. Kaoru Ishikawa, Japan's foremost authority in this field. Shortly after its publication in 1981, his book hit the best seller list for business books, being adopted as the fundamental manual for starting and operating a sound total quality control program. "Through total quality control with the participation of all employees, including the president, any company can create better products (or service) at a lower cost, increase sales, improve profit, and make the company into a better organization," says Dr. Ishikawa. Japanese executives have taken this message very seriously, and they have increased profits and improved attitudes in their companies to prove their point.

Can the Ishikawa method be imported to the United States to help American companies achieve the same results? The answer is in the affirmative. Quality control was an American invention and now has a universal application.

QC has done better, however, in its Japanese manifestation. There are several reasons for this. The Japanese have insisted on participation by all, from the chief executive officer down to line workers, while in the United States QC has often been delegated to QC specialists and consultants. In Japan the commitment is total and is "forever." According to Dr. Ishikawa, TQC must be continued as long as the company is in existence; one cannot turn the spigot on and off at will. Once begun, the movement must be continuously promoted and renewed. "Patience is a virtue," says an Oriental proverb. The meaning of that saying is worth pondering when a company intends to begin its QC activities.

The advantages of quality control are many:

- It provides true quality assurance. It is possible to build quality at every step in every process and attain 100 percent defect-free production. This is achieved through process control. It is not enough just to find defects and flaws and to correct them. What one must do is determine the causes which create these defects and flaws. TQC and process control can help workers to identify and then remove these causes.

- TQC opens up channels of communication within a company, filling it with a breath of fresh air. TQC allows companies to discover a failure before it turns into a disaster, because everyone is accustomed to speaking to one another truthfully, frankly, and in a helpful manner.
- TQC makes it possible for the product design and manufacturing divisions to follow the changing tastes and attitudes of customers efficiently and accurately so that products can be manufactured to meet customer preference consistently.
- TQC fosters probing minds that can detect false data. It can help companies to avoid relying on false sales figures and false production figures. "Knowledge is power," and that is what TQC can provide.

These and other advantages Dr. Ishikawa describes have been obtained through more than three decades of actual observation. Dr. Ishikawa does not have much use for theories, such as Theories X, Y, or Z. In their place, he gives his practical advice; for example, "The next process is your customer." He used this slogan back in the 1950s to resolve fierce hostility between workers from different production processes of a steel mill. He still uses it today in his lifelong effort to break through the barriers of sectionalism in business organizations.

Born in 1915 into the family of a prominent industrialist (his father was later to become the first president of the powerful Keidanren, or Federation of Economic Associations), Dr. Ishikawa graduated from Tokyo University in 1939 with a degree in applied chemistry. As a professor of engineering at his alma mater, he discovered the importance of statistical methods. In 1949 he became closely connected with the promotion of quality control. Since that time, he has helped many Japanese companies attain their present prominence through the application of QC. His life and the history of QC in Japan are inseparable. I shall, however, leave it to him to describe his own involvement with QC in Chapter 1. Currently, Dr. Ishikawa is president of Musashi Institute of Technology and is the most sought after QC consultant in Japan. He has also heeded the calls of a number of major United States companies, including most recently Ford Motor Company.

Chapter 2 contains an essay on the differences between QC as practiced in Japan and in the West, particularly in the United States. Inasmuch as QC was started in the United States, but has taken hold more firmly in Japan than elsewhere, Dr. Ishikawa has attempted to find some sociological and cultural explanations. He suggests that Japan's use of the *kanji* script (Chinese characters) may have helped in the promotion of QC, reasoning that the difficulty of learning the *kanji* has fostered the habit of diligent work, which is indispensable to successful QC. He goes on to say that *kanji* nations, such as Taiwan, South Korea, and the People's Republic of China, are therefore well-suited to developing good QC programs. This proposition is of course open to question. Professor John K. Fairbank, a noted scholar on China, for example, would argue that the tyranny of the written script in traditional China was one of the factors stifling that nation's development. My own criticism of this proposition is that by emphasizing the *kanji* culture Dr. Ishikawa may have neglected other more plausible explanations.

A more controversial element of Dr. Ishikawa's discussion is his inclusion of the classical debate over whether man is by nature good or evil. Quality control functions best where there is a sense of mutual trust. If man is by nature good, then that trust can always be cultivated. Dr. Ishikawa believes that Eastern civilization has always sided with the view that man is by nature good. He speculates that it is because Christianity has always sided with the view that man is by nature evil, that QC has not succeeded in the West.

Dr. Ishikawa's comment on the nature of Western civilization in this instance is off the mark. The Old Testament view of man is that he is created in the image of God and is good. Sin entered the world because of man's disobedience, but it does not follow that man remains in a state of depravity. The act of redemption through Christ allows man to be regenerated and become a "new man." If we are to follow Dr. Ishikawa's thinking process as outlined in Chapter 2, Christian nations show an equal potential for growth in QC activities as Eastern nations. Dr. Ishikawa's attempt to identify the *kanji* culture and the philosophy that man is by nature good as the reasons for QC's success reminds me of Max Weber's attempt to identify Protestant ethic with the rise of capitalism in the West. The spread of capitalism to Japan and other non-Calvinist countries has proven Max Weber wrong. The practice of QC beyond the borders of Japan and its neighboring Pacific nations should also prove Dr. Ishikawa wrong in these particular assumptions.

However, we must take Dr. Ishikawa's criticism of our continued reliance on Taylorism seriously. Managers and engineers establish work standards under Taylorism, and line workers simply obey the commands. Have we not treated our workers for too long as exchangeable and expendable commodities? It is dehumanizing both for the workers and for those who oversee them, and it creates cause for labor unrest and dissension. In its place, Dr. Ishikawa speaks of respect for humanity and of treating each worker as a whole person.

He wishes management to be more self-critical. Like Dr. W. Edwards Deming, who has given his name to the most prestigious QC award in Japan, Dr. Ishikawa says, "Whenever mistakes occur, two-thirds to four-fifths of responsibility rests with the management." That reflective approach will create a sense of trust among the workers and a significant change in their attitudes. It will insure a fresh start toward establishing true "industrial democracy."

As Dr. Ishikawa aptly remarks, quality control is a thought revolution in management. Some Japanese writers speculate that its impact may be just as great as the impact the replacement of hand tools with power-driven machines had on the first industrial revolution. Chapters 3 through 11 contain the nuts and bolts of how quality control programs may be initiated and administered. I especially wish to call your attention to Chapter 9, which deals with company relations with suppliers and subcontractors. It cautions us against a hasty adoption of the Japanese management system. For example, Toyota's "just-in-time" system of supplying parts has been regarded as one of the most effective control systems worthy of emulation. Yet it is common knowledge that some American automakers who have trimmed their supplies are finding it necessary to curtail production during peak demand periods. Why? Because they have not had adequate preparation for executing the "just-in-time" system. Quality control across the board, both within the company and among the suppliers, will eliminate the type of problem just discussed.

This book can be used as a checklist to examine your own company's readiness to engage in quality control and other attendant duties. Read only one chapter at a time and reflect carefully on the conditions existing in your company. Ask your colleagues to do likewise. The message is simple and down-to-earth. Yet in spite of its simplicity, it contains a lot of suggestions and dos and don'ts for your company. One of the best recommendations for this book comes from an IBM Japan executive, who has been engaged in QC for over two years. He said to me, "You know, every time I read this book, I gain a little more information and sophistication for the handling of our QC activities." It is a good book to have at one's side.

"With this book, I hope America's quality control activities will develop even further." Dr. Ishikawa wishes me to convey that message to his American readers. I remember telling him, "Well, Dr. Ishikawa, we may beat you at your own game." It is, of course, to be a friendly competition. Instead of talking about increasing quotas, extending voluntary restrictions, or passing local content legislation, how much nicer it would be if we simply competed to enhance our productivity through quality control! What if we applied the principles of quality control to our schools and government and to other service sectors? Think of the improvement in our educational standards and the governmental efficiency that could be realized. In fact, we may even be able to trim the Federal deficit and eliminate waste in the government as suggested by the Grace Commission report. With that happy thought, we now join Dr. Ishikawa's circle.

David J. Lu
Milton, Pennsylvania

TRANSLATOR'S ACKNOWLEDGMENT

I am indebted to the author, Dr. Ishikawa, and to the members of IBM Japan's TQC promotion team for reading and commenting extensively on my translated version. The team, known as the Customer Satisfaction Program Promotion Division, is headed by Shintaro Morita. In addition to Mr. Morita, I am especially indebted to team members Toshio Minemura and Koichi Chikugo for their valuable suggestions. I also thank Takeo Shiina and Makio Naruse, president and managing director, respectively, of IBM Japan; Haruko Mitsuaki and K. Arai of the Union of Japanese Scientists and Engineers (JUSE); Bette Schwartzberg and Judy Dorn of Prentice-Hall; and last, but not least, my wife Annabelle.

D. L.

Table of Contents

What Is Total
Quality Control?
The Japanese Way

CHAPTER I

My Encounter
With Quality Control

Total quality control, Japanese style, is a thought revolution in management.

If TQC is implemented company-wide, it can contribute to the improvement of corporate health and character.

As industry progresses and the level of civilization rises, quality control bccomes more and more important.

My wish is to see the Japanese economy become well established through QC and TQC and through Japan's ability to export good and inexpensive products world-wide. It will then follow that the Japanese economy will be placed on a firmer foundation, Japan's industrial technology will become well-established, and Japan will be in a position to engage in the export of technology on a continuous basis. As for companies, I hope they can share their profits with consumers, employees, shareholders, and society in general. I hope these companies can become instruments for enhancing the quality of life not only of the Japanese but also of all peoples, and in this way help bring about peace in the world.

I. GETTING INVOLVED IN QUALITY CONTROL

It may be somewhat presumptuous to write about myself from the outset, but in order to make clear the aim of this book it seems appropriate to explain how I became involved in quality control (QC) activities.

After my graduation from the Department of Applied Chemistry at the University of Tokyo in March 1939, I was employed by a company engaged in coal liquefaction, which was one of the national priorities in those days, and obtained experience in the fields of design, construction, operations, and research. From May 1939 through May 1941, I was commissioned as a naval technical officer with responsibilities in gunpowder. The navy was a great training ground for a young officer. During my twenty-four month tour of duty, ten months were spent in education and training. After that was over, I was placed in charge of 600 workers and was ordered to begin construction of a factory on a 245-acre site. This happened only two years after my graduation. The eight years I spent in industry and in the navy proved to be invaluable background for engaging in QC activities in later years.

In 1947 I returned to the University of Tokyo. Whenever I conducted experiments in my laboratory, however, I was faced with the problem of widely scattered data, which made it impossible to reach correct conclusions. So I began studying statistical methods in 1948.

In 1949, I heard that the Union of Japanese Scientists and Engineers (JUSE) had materials on statistical methods, and went there asking to see them. There a Mr. Kenichi Koyanagi, senior managing director of JUSE, insisted that unless I joined the QC research group and became one of its instructors he could not agree to my using their materials. My response was simple: "How could a beginner become an instructor?" But Mr. Koyanagi was very persuasive: "We are just beginning, so don't worry." In this way I was forced to join the QC activities. Once I began studying statistical methods and QC, however, I became fascinated by them. They would definitely contribute to Japan's economic recovery. With such thinking I became a serious student of QC.

The steps I took and the thought processes which guided me were the following:

1. Engineers, who pass judgment based on their experimental data, must know statistical methods by heart. I created a course entitled "How to Use Experimental Data" and made it a required course for first-semester seniors in the Faculty of Engineering at the University of Tokyo.
2. Japan does not have an abundance of natural resources and must import raw materials and foodstuffs from overseas. This means that exports must be expanded. The days of cheaply produced, poor quality goods for export are over. Japan must endeavor to make high quality goods at low cost. For that reason, quality control and statistical quality control must be conducted with utmost care.
3. The eight years that I spent in the nonacademic world after my graduation taught me that Japanese industry and society behaved very irrationally. I began to feel that by studying quality control, and by applying QC properly, the irrational behavior of industry and society could be corrected. In other words, I felt that the application of QC could accomplish revitalization of industry and effect a thought revolution in management.

Thus began my involvement with QC. I have been engaged in this field for more than thirty years, and the results have been most gratifying.

II. QUALITY CONTROL ANNUAL CONFERENCE

The first Deming Prize was awarded in September 1951 in Osaka. A quality control conference was held on that occasion, and this meeting became the first recognized QC Annual Conference in Japan.

In 1952 I served as a director of the Chemical Society of Japan. Since QC activities had some bearing on the activities of various academic associations, I appealed to these academic associations to establish an executive committee for QC conferences, and to sponsor jointly QC Annual Conferences. The Union of Japanese Scientists and Engineers was asked to handle business affairs. Each year in November, in concurrence with the awarding of the Deming Prizes, an annual conference was held to hear reports submitted by the industries. This eventually evolved into today's QC Annual Conference for Manager and Staff.

In 1962 the QC Annual Conference for Foreman and the QC Annual Conference for Consumer were initiated. The following year, the QC Annual Conference for Top Management was begun. No other country in the world holds as many varieties of QC conferences as Japan. Japan also has the honor of having the highest number of reports on QC application examples. I believe the discussions and the mutual development stemming from these conferences have been the key factors in the advancement of Japan's QC activities.

III. QUALITY MONTH AND Q MARK (Q FLAG)

To celebrate the tenth anniversary of the publication of the journal *Statistical Quality Control,* the movement called "quality month" began. At first there was talk of naming it "quality control month," but the term "control" was dropped. To be successful the movement would have to include consumers, and it was felt that the less said about "control," the more likely consumers would be to participate in it.

At the same time it was decided to create a symbol and a flag for quality control. Mrs. Haruko Mitsuaki (currently managing director of the Nikka Giken Publishing Company) took charge of the project. Professor Yoji Yamawaki of the Tokyo National University of Fine Arts and Music held a contest among his students and several designs were chosen. The one that was finally approved had the same design as today's Q mark, except that the color was the same blue as the flag of the United Nations. There was only one difficulty; the blue dye was not colorfast. How could the flag symbolizing quality show aging in its coloring? We studied the problem and surveyed the field. The solution was to make the color the same red as in Japan's national flag. The dye industry guaranteed durability of the color used in the national flag, and the quality of the Q flag could thus be guaranteed.

The Quality Month Movement conducts many activities that are suggested by the Quality Month Committee. The committee is responsible for deciding the theme and motto for the month, publishing pamphlets, and organizing lectures in various localities. The business end is handled ably by the Union of Japanese Scientists and Engineers and the Japanese Standards Association. A large number of companies participate in this movement. They raise the quality flag in the month of November and conduct a number of meaningful activities.

The idea for Quality Month received its inspiration from the practice of "Safety Week" long prevalent in Japan. The Quality Month Movement is carried out through private initiative, and Japan is probably the only country which has maintained such a sustained effort, conducting it every year in the month of November. The

People's Republic of China in 1978 designated the month of September as its quality month. It is the only other country I know of that has adopted this concept.

IV. TWO JOURNALS, SQC AND FQC

A group of us began our quality control activities in 1949. The following year, the journal *Hinshitsu Kanri (Statistical Quality Control* or SQC) was published by the Union of Japanese Scientists and Engineers. This journal disseminated knowledge about QC and TQC (total quality control) and promoted the notion of companies and workers working together and helping each other. Starting in April 1962, a new journal named *Gemba-to-QC (Quality Control for the Foreman* or FQC) was issued, also by the Union of Japanese Scientists and Engineers, addressed mainly to shop workers and their foremen. Numerous QC circle activities were the result. The FQC journal encouraged these workers to read, to exchange information, and to strive for mutual development. As a long-time contributor to both of these journals, I can point with satisfaction to the fact that Japan could not have had successful QC and TQC without them.

V. QC CIRCLE ACTIVITIES

In the early 1950s, our training programs for shop foremen were called "workshop QC study groups." The editorial board of FQC renamed them "QC circle" activities. That was in April 1962. Since that time, these activities have spread very rapidly not only to secondary industries but also to tertiary industries.

Foreign observers make the mistake of considering Japan's QC activities to be the reason behind Japanese industry's great success. It is not *the* reason, but *one* of the important reasons for success. In any event, teams of managers, scholars, labor leaders, and governmental officials have come from overseas to study Japan's QC activities. Today there are close to fifty countries conducting QC circle-type activities. We had never thought this possible. The growth of QC is due to the efforts of many people, including editors of the two journals, QC circle regional presidents, executive secretaries, and regional secretaries, whose number now exceeds 1,000, and those people handling QC affairs in the Union of Japanese Scientists and Engineers.

There was a time when I thought that QC circle activities were possible only in those countries which had been using Chinese characters in their writing and had also been influenced by Buddhism and Confucianism. But these days one hears success stories from a wide variety of countries, so I am modifying my views. My current thinking is this:

"QC circle activities, if they are consistent with human nature, will be applicable anywhere in the world, because people are people, and there is a common bond of humanity."

I hope these activities will contribute to the peace and prosperity of the world for a long time to come.

VI. DEMING PRIZES

In 1950 Dr. W. Edwards Deming came from the United States and gave a series of excellent lectures on quality control. Royalties from the book based on these lectures were made available to the Union of Japanese Scientists and Engineers, which used them to establish the Deming Prizes. These prizes included the Deming Prize (for Individual Person) and the Deming Application Prize. The Deming Prize (for Individual Person) is awarded, in principle, to an individual or individuals who have contributed to the dissemination and development of theories relating to statistical quality control. There are several different categories of the Application Prize, but it is primarily a prize given to a company which in a given fiscal year has performed exceptionally in the field of statistical quality control. Each year, as the levels of Japan's SQC and TQC rise, higher and higher standards are required of its recipients.

These prizes are the highest awards in Japan relating to SQC and TQC. The application prizes, by insisting on the highest performance, have brought about organizational overhauls in industries practicing SQC and TQC. I urge those companies engaged in SQC and TQC to apply to the prize committee and be examined for the prize within four or five years of the inception of these activities. By being examined, their SQC and TQC activities will progress even further. Of course, not everyone wins who applies for the prize, but the QC audit received in the process in itself will be a milestone, and the company's organizational structure will improve as a result.

When a company's organization becomes more efficient through SQC and TQC, and everyone looks happy with them, the prize seems to fall naturally into the company's lap. I have been involved in the work of these prizes since their inception, and the experience has proven invaluable.

VII. QC IN DIFFERENT INDUSTRIES

I have been involved in QC activities in different types of industries. My major in college was applied chemistry, and I have been a professor in chemistry-related disciplines. But my involvement with QC has been far more diverse, including such industries as the chemical, mining, metallurgical, machine, electric and electronic, textile, shipbuilding, food, and construction industries. Some of these industries mass-produce few products while others produce a small amount of each of a large number of different products. More recently, I have been involved in QC activities in finance, distribution, transportation, and service industries. It is clear to me that QC and TQC activities are basically the same, and that the same principles can be applied to different industries.

I often hear this comment: "My company is in a different category of business, so it is difficult to engage in QC or TQC. We cannot do it." My answer has remained the same: "Instead of thinking about the reasons that you cannot do, why not try to discover what you can do?"

"TQC simply means that we do what we are supposed to do."

VIII. STUDY GROUPS ON SAMPLING

Data are the basis of QC. But as soon as I began quality control activities, I discovered that in many instances data were unreliable. This was especially true in metallurgical and chemical industries where the sampling method, division method, and measurement and analysis method were inadequate. Not satisfied with just writing a book on statistically sound sampling, I established a Sampling Study Group for the Mining Industry with the help of JUSE in 1952. The group was divided into subgroups according to the following classifications: iron ore, nonferrous metal, coal, coke, sulfide ore, industrial salt, and sampling instruments. The subgroups' findings pointed the way to rationalizing the sampling method, division method, and measurement and analysis method. On the basis of these, we established Japanese Industrial Standards (JIS) for many industries. JIS also became the basis of standards established for the International Standards Organization (ISO), thus contributing to rationalization in international trade. (See the following section.)

When the issue of industrial pollution became an important concern, a Sampling Study Group for Environmental Protection was established within JUSE in 1971. It utilized the experience acquired by other study groups on sampling. It now has subgroups on air, water, and soil, and continues to study these subjects with a view to creating rational and scientific methods of sampling and analysis and measurement.

QC is often called "management by facts and data." We must approach it scientifically, know the size of errors which are inevitable, and utilize the knowledge thus acquired. Based on the experience I have gained from these study groups, I propose another principle:

"If someone shows you data obtained by the use of measuring instruments and chemical analysis, consider them suspect." (Note: Here and elsewhere quotation marks are sometimes utilized to indicate those phrases on which the author wishes to place special emphasis.)

IX. MY INVOLVEMENT WITH JIS AND ISO

I became involved with Japanese Industrial Standards in three areas:

First, I incorporated the findings of the Sampling Study Group for Mining Industry into JIS one after another, always with a view to rationalizing the sampling method, division method, and analysis method.

Second, I cooperated with various special committees of JIS on matters relating to quality control.

Third, in implementing quality control in various industries, it became clear that the existing Japanese Industrial Standards were not adequate or accurate. In 1956 those of us who were concerned with this problem set up a Committee to Rationalize Standards within the Japanese Standards Association. It studied JIS's standards for each product and incorporated its findings in a recommendation entitled "On Japanese Industrial Standards," and submitted it to Ichiro Ishikawa, then the Chairman of the Japanese Industrial Standards Committee in 1961. One of the conclusions reached at that time was that "not a single JIS standard was satisfactory." Because analysis of quality was inadequate, these standards did not spell out quality characteristics or deal adequately with substitute characteristics. They also generally set quality levels too low to satisfy the requirements of consumers. Since that time, I have been advocating the position that "quality control cannot be implemented by merely following national or international standards. These standards may be taken into consideration, but beyond these standards quality control must have the higher goals of meeting the requirements of consumers and creating quality which satisfies them."

In this manner I became closely involved in JIS's activities.

Japan had been a member nation of ISO since 1952, but my own involvement did not begin until around 1960. Up until that time Japan had not contributed to the work of ISO's technical committees, and had been criticized for this failing. We felt that we had to do something, and the work that we did in the sampling study group, described above, was chosen to become an entry in Japan's cooperative endeavor with ISO. The ISO Technical Committee No. 102, established in 1961, dealt with problems relating to iron ore. Its first subcommittee was on sampling. Japan became secretariat of these committees and completed the tasks assigned to it. International recognition received through the work in these committees was most gratifying. Japan's survival is dependent on international trade, and the country is one of the world's most advanced nations. It is my hope that Japan will be more willing to become secretariat of ISO or International Electrotechnical Commission. I hope academic circles and related industries will take note of this.

In 1969 I became a member of the ISO chapter in Japan, and since 1977 I have been its chairman. Since 1976 I have attended General Assembly and council meetings of ISO without interruption. In 1981 I became a member of ISO's executive committee and now find myself using my inadequate English to work toward international cooperation in standardization.

I have also participated in the Pacific Area Standards Congress (PASC). I can now claim a long history of involvement in international industrial standardization.

X. CONTACT WITH PEOPLE OVERSEAS

My first contact with people from overseas in the postwar era began with the coming of Dr. Deming in 1950. The visit of Dr. Juran followed in 1954. My first overseas trip was to the United States in 1958, where I served as sub-leader of a quality control study team sponsored by the Japan Productivity Center. (The team leader was Mr. Noboru Yamaguchi, then director of manufacturing, Toshiba.) We stayed in the United States from January to April. Since that time I have visited more than thirty countries, mostly on QC-related and industrial standardization activities, usually in conjunction with ISO work.

In terms of QC, I had a twofold aim in going overseas. One was to observe these good points of industry in foreign countries and adapt them for use in Japan, and the other was to let foreigners know about the good points of Japan's QC activities. During my 1958 visit to the United States with Mr. Hajime Karatsu (presently managing director,

Matsushita Communications Industry), I was able to help a number of less advanced American industries. Since 1965 I have been actively engaged in promoting Japan's QC methods in foreign countries, while also directing QC activities at home. After these experiences, I have been able to say to people overseas that they can buy products made in Japan with confidence. I believe that in this way I have indirectly aided Japan's export drive.

In the 1970s I received many requests from a number of different countries, East and West, North and South alike, asking me to conduct seminars on Japanese QC methods. Despite my poor language abilities, I lectured and conducted seminars. In May 1980, NBC carried a program entitled, "If Japan Can, Why Can't We?" which introduced to the American audience the advantages of Japanese QC. After that, the Japanese media began to write a great deal about Japanese QC. This is a sad commentary on Japan's mass media, demonstrating that they are behind the times. Knowledgeable people around the world actually began to recognize the strengths of Japan's TQC and QC circle activities in the late 1960s. These days, an average of one team a week comes from overseas to Japan to observe Japan's QC activities. Japan's country-wide quality control and QC circle activities are booming. I have become friends with many of the people who have visited us, and have learned from them also.

As discussed earlier, I served as a member of the secretariat of ISO's iron ore sampling subcommittee. Since it was an international committee, I decided that its meetings should be held in as many different countries as possible. Aside from Japan, its meeting sites included India, the USSR, West European countries, the United States, Canada, Brazil, Australia, and the Union of South Africa. In this manner the subcommittee has done its share in promoting international understanding.

From 1970 on, many seminars on quality control have been held in Japan. I conducted many such seminars for the benefit of people from developing countries. I have visited the People's Republic of China rather frequently since 1973 and I am now an advisor to the Chinese Association for Quality Control. I am also an honorary member of comparable organizations in Great Britain, the Philippines, and Argentina.

For those of us involved in quality control a number of years ago, the creation of an international organization dedicated to QC was a desirable goal. In 1966 I became a member of a preparatory committee for such an international organization. In 1969 the first International

Conference on Quality Control was held in Tokyo, and the International Academy for Quality was established. I have been an officer of this organization and have served in various capacities. IAQ meets once every three years, and its conference site is alternated between Japan, the United States, and Europe, in that order.

As I look back on my life with QC, the following becomes my hope and prayer: "That QC and QC circle activities be spread everywhere in the world, that quality all over the world be improved, that cost be lowered, that productivity be increased, that raw materials and energy be saved, that peoples all over the world be happy, and that the world prosper and be peaceful."

Many so-called management techniques were imported to Japan after the Second World War. Of these, only quality control was fully naturalized to become Japan's very own, experienced great success, and was transformed into a "new product" to be widely exported to nations overseas.

Thank you for bearing with me in this rather lengthy introduction about my own experience with QC. Whatever I am going to say is based on this experience. This is the reason for this introduction, and I thank you for your indulgence.

CHAPTER II

Characteristics of Japanese Quality Control

Quality control is to do what is to be done in all industries.

Quality control which cannot show results is not quality control. Let us engage in QC which makes so much money for the company that we do not know what to do with it!

QC begins with education and ends with education.

To implement TQC, we need to carry out continuous education for everyone, from the president down to line workers.

QC brings out the best in everyone.

When QC is implemented, falsehood disappears from the company.

I. A SHORT HISTORY OF TOTAL QUALITY CONTROL

Modern quality control, or statistical quality control (SQC), as we know it today, began in the 1930s with the industrial application of the control chart invented by Dr. W. A. Shewhart of the Bell Laboratories.

The Second World War was the catalyst that made the control chart's application possible to various industries in the United States when mere reorganization of production systems proved inadequate for meeting the exigencies of semi-wartime and wartime conditions. By utilizing quality control, however, the United States was able to produce military supplies inexpensively and in large quantity. The wartime standards published at that time became known as Z-1 Standards.

Dr. W. A. Shewhart

England also developed quality control at a relatively early date. It had been the home of modern statistics, the application of which was evident in the adoption of British Standards 600 in 1935 based on E. S. Pearson's statistical work. Later, U.S. Z-1 Standards were adopted in their entirety as British Standards 1008. Other standards were also formulated and put into use in England during the war years.

America's wartime production was quantitatively, qualitatively, and economically very satisfactory, owing in part to the introduction of statistical quality control, which also stimulated technological advances. One might even speculate that the Second World War was won by quality control and by the utilization of modern statistics. Certain statistical methods researched and utilized by the allied powers were so effective that they were classified as military secrets until the surrender of Nazi Germany.

Japan had knowledge of the early British Standards 600 in the prewar years and had them translated into Japanese during the war. A number of Japanese scholars also began studying modern statistics in earnest, but their work was expressed in mathematical language difficult to understand, and could not achieve popular acceptance.

In management Japan also lagged behind, using the so-called Taylor method in certain quarters. (The Taylor method required workers to follow the specifications set forth by specialists, and was considered a modern approach in those days.) Quality control was totally dependent on inspection, and not every product was sufficiently inspected. In those days Japan was still competing with cost and price but not with quality. It was literally still the age of "cheap and poor" products.

Introduction of Statistical Quality Control

Japan was devastated by the defeat in the Second World War. Practically all of its industries were destroyed, and there was no food, clothing, or housing. The people were close to starvation.

When the U.S. occupation forces landed in Japan, they were immediately faced with a major obstacle: failure in telephone service was all too common. The Japanese telephone was not a reliable tool for communication. The problem was not merely due to the war that had just been fought; the quality of equipment was uneven and poor. Knowing these defects, the U.S. forces ordered the Japanese telecommunication industry to begin the use of modern quality control, and took steps to educate the industry. This was the beginning of statistical quality control in Japan, May 1946.

The U.S. occupation forces taught Japanese industry straight out of the American method without making any modifications appropriate for Japan. This created some problems, but the results were rather promising, and the American method quickly spread beyond the telecommunication industry.

JIS Mark

During this period the national standards system came into being. The Japanese Standards Association was established in 1945, followed by the Japanese Industrial Standards Committee in 1946. The Industrial Standardization Law went into effect in 1949. The Japanese Agricultural Standards Law (JAS) was promulgated in 1950, and at the same time the JIS marking system was instituted based on the Industrial Standardization Law.

The JIS marking system allows certain merchandise to bear the JIS mark if made by those factories which produce designated items under the JIS standards for statistical quality control and quality assurance.

This system was instrumental in introducing and popularizing statistical quality control in Japanese industries. The system was unique in that participation in it was strictly voluntary and not by the command of the government. A company could ask to have its products inspected or choose not to have them inspected. And once passing the inspection, it could decide on its own whether or not to place the JIS mark. In foreign countries, the use of approved marks is often compulsory. In Japan, fortunately, that rule is absent. Except in those areas in which life and safety are directly threatened, I firmly believe that governmental intervention should be kept at a minimum.

Quality Control Research Group

The Union of Japanese Scientists and Engineers (JUSE) is a private organization formed by engineers and scholars in 1946. In 1949 JUSE established the Quality Control Research Group (QCRG) with members drawn from universities, industries, and government. Its aim was to engage in research and dissemination of knowledge of quality control. The members sought a means of rationalizing Japanese industries, of exporting quality products overseas, and of raising the living standards of the Japanese people. To accomplish this, they wanted to apply quality control to Japanese industries.

The Quality Control Research Group conducted its first QC Basic Course in September 1949. It met three days each month for a year, a total of thirty-six days, with engineers from industries as the primary audience. (When the second QC Basic Course was offered, the meeting schedule was modified to six days each month for a period of six months. Today the basic course still runs for six months, but meets only five days each month.) When we held the first basic course, we had the American and British standards described above translated into Japanese, and used them as texts.

After conducting the first course, it became clear to us that physics, chemistry, and mathematics are universal and are applicable anywhere in the world. However, in the case of quality control, or in anything that has the term "control" attached to it, human and social factors are strongly at work. No matter how good the American and British methods may be, they cannot be imported to Japan as they stand. To succeed, we had to create a Japanese method. Thus from the second basic course on, the QCRG staff members wrote their own texts, avoiding the use of translated works.

Seminar by Dr. Deming

In 1950 JUSE held a seminar with Dr. W. Edwards Deming of the United States as the lecturer. It was a seminar on statistical quality control for managers and engineers, and lasted eight days. The outline of the Deming seminar was as follows:

1. How to use the cycle of Plan, Do, Check, Action (PDCA, the so-called Deming cycle, relating to design, production, sales, survey, and redesign) to enhance quality.
2. The importance of having a feel for dispersion in statistics.
3. Process control through the use of control charts and how to use them.

The lectures were clear and incisive, benefiting not only the sponsors but also all those who heard Deming. A special one-day seminar for company presidents and top managers took place in Hakone, making top-level managers realize the importance of quality control for their companies.

Dr. W. E. Deming

Dr. Deming, a recognized scholar in the field of sampling, is the one who introduced quality control to Japan. He is also a good friend of Japan who knows Japan. His initial visit was followed by visits in 1951 and 1952. Since then, he has come to Japan frequently and has continued to educate the Japanese public and industry in quality control.

A Period of Overemphasis on Statistical Quality Control

In the 1950s modern quality control or statistical quality control became fashionable in Japanese factories, and the use of statistical methods, such as control charts and sampling inspection, was widespread. However, in practice it created a number of problems.

1. Experienced workers who had always relied on their experiences and common sense complained that they could not use statistical methods. They argued, often emotionally, that such methods were useless.
2. To manage a factory, companies needed to have standards set for the levels of technology, work, and inspection. They were not available. Even if someone attempted to set standards, people complained that "There are too many factors to consider. We simply cannot put these down on paper as technical standards," or "We can manage the factory without those standards anyway."
3. Data were needed to implement quality control. But there was simply a dearth of data.
4. In collecting data, the sampling method and the method of division were not followed properly. Hence even when data were available, they were seldom useful.
5. In order to collect data, measuring devices and automatic recorders were sometimes installed. In some instances, workers suspected that these devices were put there to monitor their work and destroyed them.

These were, of course, the same problems that Japanese factories had experienced even before the Second World War. But the fault was also on the side of those of us who wanted to promote modern quality control. This experience taught us the following:

1. It is true that statistical methods are effective, but we overemphasized their importance. As a result, people either feared or disliked quality control as something very difficult. We overeducated people by giving them sophisticated methods where, at that stage, simple methods would have sufficed.
2. Standardization progressed in the areas of product standards, raw material standards, technical standards, and work standards, but it remained pro forma. We created specifications and standards, but seldom made use of them. Many people felt that standardization meant using regulations to bind people.

3. Quality control remained a movement among engineers and workers in factories. Top and middle-level managers did not show much interest. A misconception was also that if a company started a quality control movement, it would cost money. In those days, we used to say, "Who is going to put a leash on the fat cat (top managers)?" Those of us who were members of the Quality Control Research Group tried to persuade top managers to join, but perhaps because of our relative youth our efforts were met with little visible success.

Dr. J. M. Juran's Visit to Japan

Help was obviously needed at that time. Fortunately, Dr. J. M. Juran responded to the invitation of JUSE and came to Japan for the first time in 1954. He conducted seminars for top and middle-level managers, explaining to them the roles they had to play in promoting QC activities.

Japanese managers had shown little understanding or interest when those young Quality Control Research Group members explained QC to them, but Dr. Juran, with his worldwide reputation, was more persuasive.

Dr. J. M. Juran

Dr. Juran's visit marked a transition in Japan's quality control activities from dealing primarily with technology based in factories to an overall concern for the entire management. There is a limit to statistical quality control which has engineers as its prime movers. The Juran visit created an atmosphere in which QC was to be regarded as a tool of management, thus creating an opening for the establishment of total quality control as we know it today.

Importance of Quality Assurance in Newly Developed Products

Quality assurance must be strictly adhered to during the stages in which new products are being developed. This realization was a turning point for us and suggested new approaches to guide our actions in the late 1950s.

Quality control or quality assurance in its initial development began with the notion that inspection has to be emphasized. In order not to ship defective products, inspection has to be done well. (Incidentally, this is still the dominant practice in the United States and Western Europe.) However, shortly after the introduction of quality control to Japan in the postwar years, we abandoned this approach. If defective products are produced at different stages of the manufacturing process, even strict inspection cannot eliminate them. If instead of relying on inspection, we produce no defective products from the very beginning—in other words, if we control the factors in a particular process which cause defective products—we can save a lot of the money that is expended for inspection. Is it wise to buy a lot of cold remedy because one is prone to catch a cold? The right kind of prevention is to make the body strong so that it is less susceptible to colds.

Having decided that this was the right approach, we consistently advocated quality assurance which emphasized control of the manufacturing process throughout the postwar years. Essentially this is still the view we hold, but lately we have begun to feel that it is still inadequate, as we discover that quality standards are constantly raised to match consumers' higher expectations.

No matter how ardently the manufacturing division tries, the issues of product reliability, safety, and economy cannot be resolved if the design is faulty or the material is poor. To solve these problems, all processes involved in developing, planning, and designing a new product must be placed under control. A quality control program which is wider in application than that of the past is required. This matter will be treated fully in Chapter 4.

Necessity of Total Involvement in Quality Assurance

If quality assurance is to be implemented at the very beginning of the developmental stage of a new product, it means that all divisions of a given company and all of its employees must participate in quality control.

When quality control emphasizes only inspection, only one division has to be involved—either the inspection division or the quality control division, and all they have to do is stand at the exit and guard it in such a way as to prevent defective products from being shipped. If a quality control program emphasizes the manufacturing process, however, involvement is extended to assembly lines, to subcontractors, and to the divisions of purchasing, production engineering, and marketing. In a more advanced application of quality control, a third phase, all of the above becomes insufficient. Participation must become company-wide. This means that those who are involved in new product planning, design, and research, those who are in the manufacturing division, and those who are in the divisions of accounting, personnel, and labor relations must, without exception, participate.

In this third phase the marketing division must play a significant role because it is the "window" through which the opinions of consumers can be heard. These opinions must be incorporated from the outset in the planning stages of the product if the product is to answer the true needs of the consumers. I shall discuss this in greater detail in later chapters.

Quality assurance must ultimately reach this third phase of development, which is implementation of quality assurance at the earliest stages of product development. At the same time, quality control has moved in the direction of total participation, involving all divisions and all employees. The convergence of these two trends has created company-wide quality control, the most important feature of Japan's QC today.

Birth of the QC Circle

In manufacturing high quality products with full quality assurance, the roles played by workers must not be overlooked. Workers are the ones who actually produce, and unless workers and their foremen are good at what they do, QC also cannot progress.

In this sense, QC education for workers is very important. In the 1950s, however, it was considered to be practically impossible.

It was not difficult to educate engineers and staff members through various seminars and conferences, but there were simply too many foremen and group leaders to handle. These were also scattered across the country. It was not easy to start educating them.

We solved that problem by utilizing the mass media, and began a QC correspondence course for foreman in 1956 through the Japan Shortwave Broadcasting Corporation. In 1957 the Japan Broadcasting Corporation (NHK) agreed to broadcast our programs as part of its educational programming. The program was well received by the public, and the text sold 110,000 copies, far exceeding the expectation of NHK. As a sequel to this success, JUSE published a monograph entitled *A Text on Quality Control for the Foreman (A and B)* in 1960, and it continues to sell well.

As part of its tenth anniversary celebration, the journal *Statistical Quality Control* published three special issues in March 1960, one for foremen, one for consumers, and one for high school teachers. The one for foremen was especially well received.

In November 1961 the *Statistical Quality Control* issued a special supplement for foremen in the workplace and called for an open-ended discussion session *(zadankai)* with participation from foremen from various industries. At one such meeting they unanimously recommended that we publish a new journal to answer their needs. Thus was born a journal entitled *Gemba-to-QC (Quality Control for the Foreman* or FQC), and the first issue was published in April 1962.

In publishing this journal we advocated that quality control activities be conducted under the name of the QC circle. There were two reasons for this.

The first was that most foremen were not in the habit of studying. Even if we created a journal for them, we had no guarantee that they would read it. If they could be expected to study on their own, at least they could be encouraged to help one another and stimulate one another's thinking. The solution was to form groups to read this journal on a rotating basis and to insure continuity. (People who are not familiar with QC activities consider QC groups to be the ones that are organized primarily to improve working conditions. This is wrong. These groups are organized for the purpose of studying; and they study to avoid making recurring mistakes.)

The second was that reading alone would not do much good for QC. Whatever was studied would have to be implemented in each person's workplace. The simple statistical methods people learned from the journal should be applied in their actual work situations. They should be encouraged to solve problems arising in the workplace both on their own and with the help of others. For this reason, group activities were far more desirable.

At that time, we emphasized the following:

1. Voluntarism. Circles are to be created on a voluntary basis, and not by a command from above. Begin circle activities with those people who wish to participate.
2. Self-development. Circle members must be willing to study.
3. Mutual development. Circle members must aspire to expand their horizons and cooperate with other circles.
4. Eventual total participation. Circles must establish as their ultimate goal full participation of all workers in the same workplace.

To create further opportunities for mutual development, the QC Annual Conference for Foremen was organized in 1962 and followed by the formation of the QC Circle Conference the next year.

It was tough going at first, and QC activities did not have many adherents. As of April 1965, three years after the initial push, only 3,700 groups were registered with us as practicing QC activities. Our insistence on voluntarism had obviously worked against us.

In retrospect, however, it was good that we made progress in this fashion. In order for the movement to endure, compulsion must be avoided and voluntarism stressed. In the long run, it is better to have gradual progress than to experience the failures that resulted when the movement was commanded from the top. Sometimes the circuitous route is the road to success. In my own experience, the initial lull was followed by a torrent of acceptance. As some QC circles showed signs of great success, companies who did not have them quickly followed suit to imitate them. I have observed similar occurrences in the United States and Western Europe, where I have been helping companies establish QC circles.

II. JAPANESE EXPERIENCE VS. WESTERN EXPERIENCE

There are many differences between the QC activities in Japan and those in the United States and Western Europe. This is due in part to each nation's unique social and cultural background. QC activities cannot be conducted in a social and cultural vacuum. They develop within the framework of different societies and cultures.

I would like to add my own thoughts on these differences, fourteen points in all, as they may be of help in understanding Japan's QC activities.

1. Professionalism

In the United States and Western Europe, great emphasis is placed on professionalism and specialization. Matters relating to QC therefore become the exclusive preserve of QC specialists. When questions are raised concerning QC, people belonging to other divisions will not answer. They will simply refer the questions to those who handle QC.

In Western countries, when a QC specialist enters a company, he is immediately put in the QC division. Eventually he becomes head of a subsection, a section, and then of the QC division. This system is effective in nurturing a specialist, but from the point of view of the entire business organization, it is more likely to produce a person of very limited vision.

For better or for worse, in Japan little emphasis is placed on professionalism. When an engineer enters a company, he is rotated among different divisions, such as design, manufacturing, and QC. At times, some engineers are even placed in the marketing division. This system may not create professionals with the highest competence, but I believe professionalism is a legacy of the old guild system, and has seen better days. People possess far greater abilities than professionalism is willing to give them credit for.

Academic and other associations are also organized differently in Japan. The American Society for Quality Control, for example, is an organization that protects the professional interests of QC professionals and specialists. In Japan academic associations are organized primarily for academic purposes.

2. Japan Is a Vertical Society

It has been said that Japan is a vertical society in which the relationship between those who are above and those who are below is very strong. However, proportionate to that strength is the weakness in the horizontal relationship. In Japanese business organization, those divisions which are directly involved in business activities, such as manufacturing, design, marketing, and purchasing, are usually strong, but staff divisions such as QC are relatively weak. Workers who are accustomed to listening to their division and section chiefs may turn deaf ears to suggestions made by staff members.

In Japan, if a marketing division wishes to start its own QC activities, sending QC specialists to that division is not the answer. These activities can succeed only if the division chief himself is willing to study QC and implement QC.

3. Labor Unions

In America and Europe, labor unions are organized along functional lines. For example, a shipyard in England has forty-five trade unions, such as the welders union and the plumbers union. If the welders union goes on strike, it can stop the operation of the entire shipyard even though the remaining forty-four unions are not on strike. In an extreme instance, a wildcat strike can shut down the shipyard. This system, in my view, is also a legacy of the old guild system, and it is simply archaic.

In Japan, by contrast, most unions are enterprise-wide unions. In Japanese industries, able workers receive training in a number of specialties and multi-functional workers are nurtured. This is impossible in America and Europe, where functional unions are too strong.

4. The Taylor Method and Absenteeism

Frederick W. Taylor is often called the father of scientific management, and his method is still used in the United States, Western Europe, and the Soviet Union. The Taylor method is one of management by specialists. It suggests that specialists and engineers formulate technical standards and work standards. All workers have to do is simply do what they are told to do and follow the standards set for them.

This method was probably a viable method some fifty years ago, but it is certainly not applicable to today's Japan. Fifty years ago there were few engineers, and most workers were either elementary school graduates or illiterates with no elementary school education. Under such circumstances, the Taylor method was probably effective. In today's world, where workers are well-educated and self-aware, this method cannot be imposed on them. The Taylor method does not recognize the hidden abilities workers possess. It ignores humanity and treats workers like machines. It is no wonder that workers resent being treated that way and show no interest in their work.

In the United States and Western Europe, many workers work in order to obtain a livelihood. They work because they have to, and absenteeism is rampant. In some factories, absenteeism can be as high as 15 to 20 percent. They have two days off each week, but in some instances, absenteeism for Mondays and Fridays amounts from 25 to 40 percent. This means that close to one half of the workers work only four days a week. "Why do you work only four days?" I once asked a worker. His response was, "Well, I cannot make both ends meet if I work only three days."

If people are treated like machines, work becomes uninteresting and unsatisfying. Under such conditions, it is not possible to expect products with good quality and high reliability. The rate of absenteeism and the rate of turnover are the measures one can use in determining the strengths and weaknesses of management style and worker morale in any company.

5. Elitism and Class Consciousness

In Europe, especially in England and France, there is a kind of class consciousness existing among graduates of certain universities that borders on discrimination against those who are less fortunate than they. At one French factory I asked, "What percentage of your foremen become division or section chiefs?" Division chiefs and section chiefs hesitated and did not answer. The factory manager answered in one word: "None." In France section chiefs and division chiefs are a separate breed of people from foremen.

This attitude has also had an undesirable effect on Europe's old colonial possessions. I was in Indonesia, a former Dutch colony, and met managers of Japanese companies that had been successfully doing business there. They said that they would not hire graduates of the University of Jakarta. Engineering graduates from that university without any experience immediately wanted to become managers and disliked dirtying their hands. Their elitism made them poor workers. These Japanese companies preferred to hire graduates of technical schools and give them training. They usually became better technicians and engineers.

In postwar Japan so many more students have been graduating from college than in prewar days that elitism seems to be disappearing. The only exceptions may be found among the graduates of the Faculty of Law at the University of Tokyo. Altogether this is a desirable development; elitism is something akin to the Taylor method.

6. Pay System

In the United States and Western Europe, the pay system is based on merit. It is a system which pays more to those who are more efficient than others without much regard for age. Lately Japan has also been introducing an element of merit pay in its pay system, but the dominant practice still remains one of seniority and ranking. I believe that the justification for the merit pay scheme is the notion that people can be made to work for money.

If we are to motivate people by money alone, what will happen to those people who find no satisfaction in their work? As I demonstrated earlier, if we raise their pay they may come to work only three or four days a week. This phenomenon is discernible not only in the United States and Western Europe where the pay base is high but also in developing countries. I heard that in India, if pay is raised just a little, absenteeism increases. Almost every nation in the world is concerned with the issue of changing attitudes toward work. This is why Japan is receiving so much attention.

The system of seniority and ranking does have a number of problems, of course. With the increase in life expectancy, the problem of aging workers becomes a major issue. It cannot be resolved merely by extending the retirement age, because that in turn creates more problems. Be that as it may, I think it is wrong merely to think that people can be made to work by money alone.

Joy, desire, and pleasure have many different dimensions. We must have a clear understanding of these basic human drives before we can begin to change people's attitudes toward work. I am not a specialist on these matters, so answers to these problems must be left to specialists, but let me venture an analysis here.

A. Monetary desires and the joy accompanying them fill the following basic needs:

- the minimum conditions for survival
- man's perennial quest for wealth and
- material satisfaction (for example, wanting to buy a car)

These are basic and even necessary conditions for living in society, but are not satisfactory conditions. In a sense, they represent base desires of the lowest description. People cannot be satisfied and happy with them. The present condition of the world fully illustrates their inadequacy. There are alternatives:

B. The satisfaction of doing a job well. This includes the following:

- the joy of completing a project or reaching a goal
- the joy of climbing a mountain because it is there

C. The happiness coming from cooperating with others and from being recognized by others.

Man cannot live alone. An individual lives as a societal being, as a member of a group, of a family, of a QC circle, of a company, of a city, of a nation, and of the world. Thus it becomes a matter of utmost importance for that individual to be recognized by society. In more concrete terms, it means:

- to be recognized by others
- to be able to work with others in a group situation (such as QC circle) and interact with others with friendship and love
- to be a respected member of a good nation, of a good industry, of a good workplace, etc.

D. The joy of personal growth, which includes the following:

- experiencing the satisfaction which comes from being able to utilize one's own abilities to the fullest and from growing as a person.
- having self-confidence, and becoming a self-fulfilled person
- using one's own brains, working voluntarily, and in this way contributing to society.

Of the above, I believe that B. C. and D. truly represent man's desires and requirements for happiness. Our task is to make use of these and treat people like people. If we are saddled with the notion that monetary needs are the most important, we can bring harm to individuals, societies, nations, and the whole world.

7. Turnover Rate, Layoff, and Lifetime Employment System

In the United States and Western Europe the job turnover rate is very high. A number of years ago I visited Australia and found that at one steel mill the turnover rate in the blast furnace section was 100 percent. When one speaks of a 100 percent turnover rate, it does not mean that all one hundred workers in a given section are *replaced* within one year. There are some who will quit in a month or two. What the expression "100 percent turnover rate" means is that within one year, one hundred people will be hired and will leave their posts. If the turnover rate is that bad in places like blast furnaces where experience is required, how much worse will it be in other areas? In such a work situation one cannot expect efficiency or quality.

The employment pattern in Japan is family-like, and in many instances lifetime employment is practiced. If factories are well managed, workers seldom move from one factory to another. (In sales and in small and medium size enterprises, the turnover rate is rather high, creating problems.) Instead, Japanese companies stress education and training, especially QC education. If employees are well-educated and well-trained, that fact alone can benefit both the employees and the company immensely. In the United States and Western Europe, I understand that it is very difficult to implement the same type of education and training given by Japanese companies.

In the early 1960s some Western managers with a modern outlook began to study the system of lifetime employment, with a view to introducing certain features of that system into their own companies to stabilize employment. I can recall a conversation I had with an American company president some ten years ago. "We have this many people, representing *x* percent of the employees, who have worked for us for over thirty years. And a large number for over twenty years, and again a substantial number for over ten years." He was proud of the fact that employees feel comfortable with his company and remain with it for a long time because of his good management.

Lifetime employment is, of course, a good system as long as it will not produce people who say, "I have no other choice; that's why I am putting up with this company." Once in a while it would be good to have people change jobs saying, "I can't remain in this company with the kind of president and management we have. I am worried about the future of the company. It does not allow us to do our best." I like to see people with courage, conviction, and independent minds. We must not make the lifetime employment system into a system which nurtures too many apple polishers.

If properly handled, a true lifetime employment system can be a desirable system from the points of view of humanity, democracy, and management.

8. Difference in Writing Systems—*Kanji*

The Chinese script used in Japanese writing, called *kanji,* is the most difficult writing system in the world. *Kanji* is hieroglyphic and ideographic. It is very difficult to memorize all the characters. One simply has to see how foreigners study Japanese to realize how difficult *kanji* is. Nations that use *kanji* are forced to try harder, and Japanese, Taiwanese, South Koreans, Chinese, and overseas Chinese are generally very much interested in education. In the Japanese and Korean languages, phonetic symbols are used along with *kanji,* creating unique and, in my view, the best writing systems of language. In the case of Chinese, *kanji* is used exclusively, which at times is rather inconvenient.

When QC circle activities first began in Japan, I thought they would be confined to Japan. If they should spread to foreign countries, the only places where they would succeed would be in other *kanji* nations. I felt that way because I was interested in the correlation between education and the diligence of workers, which has direct bearing on the success of QC circle activities. Lately, however, I have come to the conclusion that nations other than *kanji* nations can also succeed in these endeavors.

9. Homogeneous Nations, Multi-Racial Nations, and Foreign Workers

Japan is a nation of one race and one language. There is no other nation in the world that has only one race in a population exceeding

100 million. For example, the United States consists of many ethnic groups and includes people who cannot speak English. In Europe most nations are of a single race, but in their factories there are many foreign workers. Once when I visited a German electrical machinery factory I saw eight languages represented on a bulletin board. The factory hired workers from at least seven foreign countries. In establishing work standards, the factory had to rely on a system of communication that did not depend on spoken words. It was a difficult situation.

Being a nation of one race with a population of over 100 million people means that Japan can have an attractive domestic market. It has a number of advantages in industrial production which other nations do not possess. (Taiwan is also a nation of a single race, but its population is only 17 million and its domestic market is too small.)

10. Education

The Japanese people are very interested in education, and the use of *kanji* may be in part responsible for this interest. In the late Tokugawa period (1603–1867) the three Rs were taught widely in temple schools that were spread across the country. The love of education, thus manifested, was to become the basis of Japan's modern education system, introduced after the Meiji Restoration (1868). In the post-Second World War era Japanese parents strongly supported their children's academic endeavors. Entrance examinations to colleges were often called "examination wars," attesting to the seriousness of purpose behind them.

Lately, developing countries have joined the ranks of countries interested in education. Many countries now mandate six to nine years of compulsory education. From my own personal observation, I believe that it is dangerous to equate compulsory education and a high rate of school age children actually attending schools. In some countries, even with compulsory education the rate of attendance still falls between 30 to 70 percent, owing to the high incidence of children not finishing school. Unless parents and society both have a good understanding of the importance of education, school attendance is not likely to increase.

In Japan's case, aside from compulsory education through the ninth grade, the number of children entering higher levels of schooling, from middle school to high school, from high school to a two- or four-year college, is very high. Consequently, the people who enter the job market are literate and show high aptitude for mathematics. In Japan this is taken for granted, but this situation is rather uncommon in the world. This has made it much easier in Japan to educate people in QC and statistical methods.

QC education within industries is beginning to spread in Western countries, but such education will encounter difficulties unless the general level of education improves in these countries.

11. Religion

Religion has a very significant relation to the implementation of QC. Christianity is still dominant in the Western nations, while Islam and Hinduism continue to hold sway in developing countries. Japan is still strongly influenced by the teachings of Confucianism and Buddhism. Confucianism is divided into two strains. One is represented by Mencius, who said that man is by nature good. The other is represented by Hsuntzu, who said that man is by nature evil. I studied Confucianism from several angles, and my belief is that, with education, anyone can become good in the best tradition of Mencius.

The basic teachings of Christianity appear to say that man is by nature evil. *(Translator's note:* The translator dissociates himself from this statement. See the translator's introduction.) This teaching has cast a shadow over the Western nations' management philosophy. It suggests that people, for example employees in the manufacturing division, cannot be trusted. Therefore the divisions of inspection and quality control must be made independent and be given greater power. Without this power to observe and inspect, there can be no quality assurance. This attitude is clearly a manifestation of a theory that man is by nature evil. In some American factories the number of inspectors amounts to roughly 15 percent of all workers engaged in manufacturing. In Japan, the comparable figure is only one percent, in those factories where total quality control is well advanced. The difference is enormous.

Basically, if everything is produced without defect, there is no need for inspectors. Defects create a need for inspection. Inspection in itself is not unimportant, but in Japan we do it differently. We give the best QC education to workers in the manufacturing division, enabling them to control the production process to achieve 100 percent defect-free products. This method is based on the assumption that people are by nature good. The QC education in the manufacturing division must be conducted with care. Inspection is conducted by the workers themselves, and the manufacturing division must be responsible for its own quality assurance.

I shall deal with this issue in the chapter on quality assurance. Inspectors are people who are not really needed. If a factory has too many of them, their presence will reduce the factory's productivity and raise its cost.

12. Relationship with Subcontractors

Twenty-four or twenty-five years ago, more than one-half of Japan's subcontractors fell into the category of medium and small companies. Technologically and operationally, they were in rather poor shape. Yet the average Japanese company purchased materials approximating 70 percent of its manufacturing cost from outside suppliers. This practice was especially prevalent among assembly industries.

If the parts purchased were defective, no matter how hard the final assembler worked good products would not emerge. Knowing this, we began QC education among subcontractors in the late 1950s. We also attempted to make these subcontractors specialists in their own fields. Today, Japan's automobiles and electronics are considered to be the best in the world. This is due in part to the excellence of their parts suppliers.

In contrast, in Western countries companies try to produce all the parts they need in their own factories. In the United States companies order an average of 50 percent of their parts from subcontractors. For example, Ford Motor Company maintains its own small steel mill, fully equipped with a blast furnace in its factory. Its small scale of steel production does not permit the company to keep good engineers, and its technology suffers as a result. Ford cannot compete against Japanese steel mills, which have many engineers and export everywhere in the world. In terms of quality and cost effectiveness, there is simply no competition. This fact was recently underscored when the steelmaking division of Ford came to Japanese steel companies asking for technical cooperation.

Quite a few years back I visited a Chinese factory and was greeted by the plant manager with the boast, "My factory is a fully integrated factory." I did not understand the meaning of the term "fully integrated factory" and inquired. He responded, "We make all the parts we need within the company." I was taken aback. In the People's Republic of China, control by central and local governments was very strict. In spite of (or rather because of) this control, procurement of raw materials and parts was difficult. This might have been one of the reasons that they wanted to make a factory self-sufficient. Or they might have also been thinking about the possibility of war. However, it did not make much sense for a machine factory to build its own foundry with a thirty- or fifty-ton capacity. The amount of production was so small that it could never be operated efficiently. Nor could it assemble good technicians and engineers. A better solution would have been to build specialized factories and plan to nurture their growth.

In the summer of 1978 I met with members of the National Planning Commission and National Economic Commission of the People's Republic of China. This was the advice I gave them at that time: "I understand that China is a very large country which still lacks adequate transportation facilities. You also have to be concerned with the possibility of attack by enemies. So it may not be possible to implement the plan I am about to suggest on a nationwide basis. But may I suggest that you establish manufacturers who are specialized in their own fields at least in each of your provinces. Otherwise we cannot expect to upgrade quality or increase productivity." I am now informed that China is promoting "specialization and cooperation."

13. Democratization of Capital

There still remains in Western countries an old style of capitalism in which only a few capitalists own each company as major stockholders. In such instances, owners may directly operate the company. In recent years, however, managers are often hired from elsewhere to operate these companies. In Japan one can no longer find owner managers in large companies. After the war, there was a dissolution of *zaibatsu* (conglomerates), resulting in democratization of capital in Japan. (Owner managers still exist among medium and small size companies.)

In the West, owners hire the president of the company. The president is expected to make short-term profits and his performance is periodically checked. If he does not perform as expected, he is fired. From the president's point of view there is always a danger of being fired if profits fall even a little. Furthermore, the Securities and Exchange Commission requires that a balance sheet be made public every three months, encouraging companies to look for short-term gains. What this does to a manager is make him too sensitive to the present profit. He is ill-equipped to deal with long-term problems. The trade war between Japan and the United States on automobiles and the decline of steel mills in the United States are, in the final analysis, caused by this inability to solve long-term problems.

Japanese economy grew in the postwar years because of democratization of capital. It made it possible for companies to adopt long-term perspectives and to operate on the principle of quality first. Unless one can see from a long-term perspective, immediate profit and cost become the most important concern. Managers of major Japanese industries are relatively free from this concern and can devote their attention to their social responsibilities, including responsibilities to their employees and their families, to consumers, and to the nation in general. In the meantime, old-style capitalist managers in the West show interest only in themselves and in their own families. (In Japan some managers, usually from medium and small firms, exhibit a similar tendency, however.)

In this sense, the postwar *zaibatsu* dissolution conducted by the U.S. occupation forces was beneficial to Japan. It created a new democratic capitalism. It brought to Japan liberalism and fair distribution of income (which is a break from the Pareto curve). It thus contributed to the Japanese economic development that has lasted up to this day.

In Japan some impatient top managers want to replace their factory managers and division managers at the first sign of poor performance. This is not a desirable practice. Factory managers and marketing division managers must only be evaluated after three years on the job. Otherwise they may become people with myopic views who are only concerned with short-term profits. Woe unto those companies that let their managers forget long-term equipment rationalization.

14. The Role of the Government—No Control, Just Stimulation

Bureaucrats all over the world love control. This tendency is worse in communist countries where top-level governmental officials are seldom removed from their positions. Japan is also not free from problems, but in general I think the bureaucrats in the Ministry of International Trade and Industry have done well. My own view is that the government must provide stimulation for the private sector but never control it. Humanity is not respected in those countries where control is the norm or in developing countries where nationalism or fascism holds sway over people. These countries force their people to buy inferior products at high prices and cause suffering in the process.

Since 1960, Japan has entered an era of trade liberalization. In 1962 a long-term plan was established which set as its goal the liberalization of eighty-eight percent of total trade. Some executives spoke against this plan, but those of us who dealt with quality control positively supported the move toward liberalization. Liberalization did not have to be feared if Japan could continue to produce high-quality, low-cost products. We accepted it as a challenge and invented a slogan, "trade liberalization through quality control," and promoted QC activities. Companies entered into a phase of total quality control that involved everyone. They competed freely and fiercely (and often excessively) among themselves and became internationally competitive. By contrast, Japanese agriculture took the route of protectionism, only to lose its competitiveness entirely. This is why we eat the most expensive beef and rice in the world. The finance industry, under the guise of protecting the people, also chose the route of protectionism. Delayed rationalization is the result.

The terms commonly accepted for describing economic activities are capitalism, socialism, and communism. I prefer to use two categories, free economy and controlled economy.

Two Episodes

So far I have been talking about differences between Japan and the West. Let me illustrate the perception gap which still exists today with two stories from my own personal experience.

In June 1973 I participated in an Annual Conference sponsored by the European Organization on Quality Control held in Belgrade, Yugoslavia, along with a team of foremen. After my speech a Frenchman asked, "After hearing M. Ishikawa's speech, I now know why Japan succeeded so well through QC. Japan's success after the Second World War will provide a good role model for developing countries. Please give us some pointers that they can use."

How uninformed can one be? Japan is not a developing country. It is the country which built the battleship *Yamato* and Zero fighter planes during the Second World War. Unfortunately many Europeans still think of Japan as a developing country inhabited by "those yellow skinned people." I was hurt by the tone of that question, but answered as follows:

"In response to the question, I would like to emphasize two significant accomplishments of the Japanese people. They are education and free competition. Even before the Meiji Restoration (1868), there was a widespread system of education for common people given by temple schools. This was the foundation on which the Meiji people could build their system of compulsory education. After the Second World War, compulsory education was extended to nine years. Family members give children in school strong support. Over ninety-nine percent of children complete middle school, and more than ninety percent of students in the same age group finish high school. People are well-educated, making the task of educating employees much easier. Japanese industries have succeeded because they can provide effective and enthusiastic QC education for all employees, including top managers and assembly line workers.

"Now on the issue of free competition, I would like to point out the fact that Japan has promoted trade liberalization consistently since 1960. Japanese industries are exposed to the most fierce forms of competition imaginable both at home and abroad. In order to win, all employees, from the president on down, have learned to work together with all that they have. In contrast, many developing countries are limiting their trade in the name of nationalism. They can expect neither quality nor lower costs if they persist in this practice. Whenever I go to developing countries to teach, I tell government leaders that they must liberalize their trade step by step."

I would like to add a related story. The time: June 1981; the place: Paris, at another European Conference on Quality Control. Dr. Juran gave a special presentation on the subject "When Can the West Catch Up with Japan?"

Here is what Dr. Juran said:

"Japan has done its QC education well. But it took ten years for this education to show results, for quality to improve, and for productivity to rise. No matter how hard Western nations try to engage in QC education, they may not catch up with Japan until the 1990s, since it requires ten years for the QC education to take effect."

III. CHARACTERISTICS OF JAPANESE QUALITY CONTROL

In promoting QC activities we became increasingly aware of the differences discussed earlier existing between Japan and Western countries. Through that work I was able to identify certain characteristics of Japanese quality control, which I shall describe in this section.

After the war many control methods were introduced to Japan. However, nothing could compare with quality control in the ability to become firmly entrenched, fully implemented, and successful in Japan, and then be re-exported to the West. By fully utilizing the characteristics of Japanese quality control, Japanese products could claim the highest quality in the world and be exported all over the globe.

In December 1967 the seventh Quality Control Symposium determined that the following six characteristics were the ones which distinguished Japanese quality control from that of the West:

1. Company-wide quality control; participation by all members of the organization in quality control
2. Education and training in quality control
3. QC circle activities
4. QC audits (Deming Application Prize and presidential audit)
5. Utilization of statistical methods
6. Nationwide quality control promotion activities

These are the six characteristics of Japanese quality control; they have both advantages and disadvantages. What we try to do is to eliminate disadvantages and enhance advantages.

I shall be dealing with those items listed in 1, 3, 4, and 5 in detail in separate chapters. Here I would like to discuss the remaining two items.

Education and Training in Quality Control

I have been repeating this frequently: "Quality control begins with education and ends with education." "To promote QC with participation by all, QC education must be given to all employees, from the President to assembly line workers." "QC is a thought revolution in management, therefore the thought processes of all employees must be changed. To accomplish this, education must be repeated over and over again."

There is no other country like Japan in promoting QC education so diligently. One QC specialist from Sweden who came to study Japan's QC in 1967 could not hide his wonderment: "I am terribly impressed by the industry's enthusiasm for its employees' education. In Japan you have the lifetime employment system. The more you educate your employees, the more the company and the employees will benefit. In Sweden we have a high turnover rate. We give employees education, only to see them move to other companies. We can never promote education like Japan." These words are still fresh in my mind.

A. QC Education for Each Level.

In Japan, very detailed education programs are available for each job level, including the president, company directors, managing directors, division and section chiefs, engineers, foremen, QC circle promoters, QC circle leaders and members, and assembly line workers in addition to special courses for marketing divisions and purchasing divisions. These programs were initially organized by the Union of Japanese Scientists and Engineers. In the West, QC education is available for engineers, but seldom is education made available for other types of jobs, for example assembly line workers.

B. Long-term Education

In the West, QC education normally lasts for five to ten days. This is insufficient. The QC Basic Course designed by JUSE, which serves as the model for Japan's QC education courses, lasts for six months, meeting five days each month. Participants study for one week and then put to use what they have learned for three weeks when they return to their workplace. The data they have to use for study are found in their own workplace. Then they return to the next session of QC course instruction armed with the results of their three weeks' practice. In other words, the JUSE course is a continuous repetition of study and practice. A special instructor is assigned to give individualized lessons, even when there are only two or three participants. This kind of teaching helps not only the participants but also the instructor, who can get a sense of what is going on in different types of industry through this kind of contact. To teach is after all, the best way to be trained. Japan has continued this type of education for over thirty years. The depth of knowledge acquired in this fashion is considerable, continuously strengthening the foundation of QC activities in Japan.

C. Education and Training within the Company.

The activities described above are conducted by specialized organizations and may not answer all the needs of a given industry or company. A company may wish to choose its own program instead. In fact some companies develop their own texts and engage in their own programs of education and training for all employees.

D. Education Must Be Continued Permanently.

QC education has been conducted in Japan since 1949 without interruption. Year after year more courses have been added to the total educational effort. Every person gets older by one each year, and new employees enter an organization each year. Education must be maintained to answer the needs of the organization of its employees.

E. Formal Education Is Less Than One-Third of the Total Educational Effort.

Education does not end with assembling workers to receive formal instruction. At best, this instruction can represent only a small portion of their total education. It is the responsibility of the boss to teach his subordinates through actual work. In addition, he must learn to delegate authority to his subordinates. What he must do is provide general guidelines and then let the subordinates work voluntarily. In this way, people will grow.

In this discussion I have consistently used the expression "education and training." In the West the same concept is described by the term "industrial training," which does not provide room for "education." In the West, people seem to emphasize the training element, which is to make workers more adept in those skills which the companies can use. My feeling is that we must educate the workers. We must make them think and then change their thought patterns.

Nationwide Organizations Promoting Quality Control

The QC Research Group, Quality Month Committee, Committee for the National Conference on Quality Control, QC Circle Headquarters, and QC Circle Regional Chapters are the names of some private organizations that promote QC activities. They, and organizations similar to them, have been the motivating force contributing to the postwar development of QC activities in Japan.

The Quality Month Committee was organized in 1960 through private initiative. It selected November to be the quality month each year. Activities pertaining to QC were to be held in November on a nationwide scale to popularize QC and to enlighten the public. Today, among the main activities held during this month are the QC Annual Conference for Consumers, QC Annual Conference for Top Management, QC Annual Conference for Manager and Staff, QC Annual Conference for Foremen, and the All-Japan QC Circle Conference. After the completion of the QC Annual Conference for Top Management, the awarding of Deming prizes is made in Tokyo. In major cities of different regions, local public lecture meetings also take place.

These activities are coordinated by the Quality Month Committee. Its expenses are paid for from the proceeds of promotional texts (six to ten items) that the Committee prepares annually. This committee is also responsible for establishing the Quality Mark and for making the Quality Flag.

Quality Month is now being adopted by China and a number of other countries. But Japan remains the only country that has such a wide range of activities. What is remarkable about the Japanese effort is that not a penny of government money is involved and that participation in the Quality Month activities is strictly voluntary. On this basis significant activities have continued for over twenty years. That is what impresses visitors to Japan.

The National Meeting of Standardization was initiated in 1958. It takes place each year around October 14, the International Standardization Day, contributing to dissemination and promotion of Japan's industrial standardization and quality control.

In Japan October and November are designated Industrial Standardization Promotion Months. November is Quality Month. We combine industrial standardization and quality control and promote both of them at the same time.

No matter how many national standards are established, unless production can meet the quality standards these standards are rendered meaningless. In developing countries, some governmental officials feel that to raise the quality of their products all they have to do is establish a set of national standards. That is of course wrong. On paper, national standards may appear sound, but that alone is meaningless. Their workers must make products which can meet quality standards through implementation of QC activities, otherwise national standards will remain elusive. The keys to Japan's success have been in the simultaneous establishment of industrial standardization and national standards, along with quality control, and in the simultaneous promotion of these activities.

South Korea and China take a different approach. In both countries the government is the one which promotes total quality control and QC circle activities. There are many quality control associations in the world which are privately sponsored, but again their approach is different from that of Japan. The American Society for Quality Control, for example, is a professional organization that is primarily interested in promoting the position and income of QC specialists and in the training of such specialists. Matters of national concern, such as the issue of quality of American products, have not been adequately treated by this or other organizations. In the United States QC activities are promoted by QC specialists for the sake of their own consultant fees. The United States cannot match the type of service rendered by Japan's QC Circle Headquarters and Regional Chapters, whose staff visit companies with their own box lunches.

QC activities overseas are either the government-sponsored or commercially oriented types. Just how these activities will develop I do not know. Can they last? These are questions to be pondered.

CHAPTER III

The Essence of Quality Control

The first step in QC is to know the requirements of consumers.

Another step in QC is to know what the consumers will buy.

One cannot define quality without knowing the cost.

Anticipate potential defects and complaints.

Always consider taking appropriate action. Quality control not accompanied by action is mere avocation.

An ideal state of quality control is where control no longer calls for checking (inspection).

I. WHAT IS QUALITY CONTROL?

Japanese quality control is a thought revolution in management. It is an approach representing a new way of thinking about management.

The Japanese Industrial Standards (JIS) define quality control as follows:

"A system of production methods which economically produces quality goods or services meeting the requirements of consumers. Modern quality control utilizes statistical methods and is often called statistical quality control."

My own definition is as follows:

"To practice quality control is to develop, design, produce and service a quality product which is most economical, most useful, and always satisfactory to the consumer."

To meet this goal, everyone in the company must participate in and promote quality control, including top executives, all divisions within the company, and all employees.

Setting aside the definition, I should like to outline a number of pointers in implementing quality control:

1. We engage in quality control in order to manufacture products with the quality which can *satisfy the requirements of consumers*. The mere fact of meeting national standards or specifications is not the answer. It is simply insufficient. Japanese Industrial Standards or international standards established by the International Organization for Standardization (ISO), or International Electrotechnical Commission (IEC) are not perfect. They contain many shortcomings. Consumers may not be satisfied with a product which does meet JIS. We must also keep in mind that consumer requirements change from year to year. Generally even when industrial standards are modified, they cannot keep pace with consumer requirements.

2. We must emphasize *consumer orientation*. Heretofore it has been acceptable for manufacturers to think that they are doing consumers a favor by selling their products to them. Let us call this a "product out" type of operation. What I propose is a system of "market in" in which

consumer requirements are to be of utmost concern. In practical terms, I propose that manufacturers study the opinions and requirements of consumers, and take them into account when they design, produce, and sell their products. When developing a new product, a manufacturer must anticipate consumers' requirements and needs. There is a saying that "consumer is king." The right of selecting products rests with the consumer.

3. How one interprets the term "quality" is important. In the above definitions, it is interpreted to mean "quality of product," but here I am giving it a broader interpretation.

Narrowly interpreted, quality means quality of product.

Broadly interpreted, quality means quality of work, quality of service, quality of information, quality of process, quality of division, quality of people, including workers, engineers, managers, and executives, quality of system, quality of company, quality of objectives, etc. To control quality in its every manifestation is our basic approach.

4. No matter how high the quality, if the product is overpriced it cannot gain customer satisfaction. In other words, one cannot define quality without considering price. This is important in planning and designing quality. There can be no quality control which ignores price, profit, and cost control. The same can be said about the amount of production. If a factory cannot get hold of figures for the amount of its production, the amount of its scrap, or the number of defects or reworks needed, it will not be able to ascertain its percent defective (fraction defective) and the rework rate. Without them, it cannot engage in QC. Insufficient supply of a product which is in demand will inconvenience customers. An excessive supply will be a waste of labor, raw materials, and energy. Cost control and quality control are two sides of the same coin. To engage in effective cost control, effective quality control must be implemented. Also when control is to be extended to the amount of production, if the percent defective fluctuates, or if a lot has to be rejected, then there can be no effective production control. One must always strive to supply a product with *just quality, just price,* and *just amount.*

To engage in quality control means to

1. use control of quality as the basis.
2. engage in integrated control of cost, price, and profit.
3. control quantity (amount of production, of sales, and in stock) and date of delivery.

When all divisions and all employees of a company participate in total quality control, they must engage in quality control in its broader sense, which includes cost control and quantity control. Otherwise quality control, even in its narrow sense, cannot be accomplished. This is the reason why total quality control is also called "integrated quality control," "full-participation quality control," and "control of management quality."

II. ABOUT QUALITY

Knowing True Quality Which Conforms to Consumers' Requirements

Quality control is done for the purpose of realizing the quality which conforms to consumers' requirements. The first step in quality control is to know what this concept really means.

Previously, many Japanese industries did not have adequate answers to the following questions: "What is a good car?" "What is a good radio?" "What is a good steel plate?"

Consumers may or may not know how to respond to these questions. Engineers or those who are responsible for the operation of a factory usually come up with smart answers, such as, "If such and such figures match product standards, then the product in question can be considered good," or point to a chart and say, "Well, the product is within the tolerance limits on a drawing so it is a good one." These answers overlook the fact that product standards and tolerance limits on a drawing are quite unreliable.

In implementing QC, I give the following warnings:

- If someone shows you his product standards, treat them with skepticism.
- If someone shows you his raw material standards, treat them with skepticism.
- If someone shows you tolerance limits on a drawing, treat them with skepticism.
- If he also shows you data obtained by the use of measuring instruments and chemical analysis, consider them suspect.

It is true that product standards and analysis data and the like are very important in quality control. But people do assemble data carelessly. The first rule of thumb is to be skeptical of all data.

More than two decades ago I was engaged in studying Japanese Industrial Standards for newsprint rolls. The standards dealt with the tensile strength, thickness, and width of the newsprint roll. A person in charge of QC at a paper mill which I visited confided in me, "Sometimes we receive a lot of complaints from newspaper companies when the product fully meets the industrial standards, and at other times we receive no complaint at all when we do not meet the standards. So we simply ignore JIS standards." I asked for specifics, and he responded that the complaint most often heard was that the roll would tear while printing was taking place.

What the consumer—in this case the newspaper company—required of newsprint rolls was that the paper not tear while being printed on by a rotary press. We shall call this one of its *true quality characteristics*. In contrast, the tensile strength and thickness were merely conditions to achieve that true quality. So we shall call them *substitute quality characteristics*. The relationship between them had not been made clear at that time. (See Diagram III-1.)

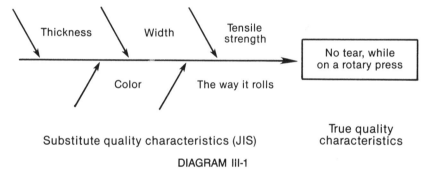

Substitute quality characteristics (JIS)   True quality characteristics

DIAGRAM III-1

For newsprint rolls, the best method of insuring quality would be to put every roll through a rotary press before shipment to see if it would tear. But this type of inspection is not possible. A given roll may or may not tear, but it cannot be determined without first using it. So at the time of shipment, inspection is conducted by using substitute quality characteristics, such as tensile strength or thickness. But this is also not an easy task.

Generally the procedure is as follows. First, one must determine the true quality characteristics of a given product and then deal with the questions of how to measure such characteristics and how to determine the product's quality standards. Once they become discernible, substitute quality characteristics which are likely to have a bearing on true quality characteristics will be chosen. Next comes the task of determining the relationship between true and substitute quality characteristics through quality analysis and through statistics. Only then can one know how much use of substitute quality characteristics can be made to satisfy true quality characteristics. To establish substitute quality characteristics, products must be tested and tested again while they are in actual use. Often this is not done adequately before national or international industrial standards (mostly substitute quality characteristics) are determined. Useless standards are the reasons for the existence of inadequate newsprint rolls. That is why I always emphasize satisfying the true requirements of the consumers rather than of national standards.

Normally the functions or capabilities of a product are part of its true quality characteristics. In the case of a good passenger car, true quality characteristics or those attributes which consumers require may include the following: good styling, easy driving, comfortable riding, good acceleration, stability at a high speed, durability, less chance of breakdown, easy repair, and safety. So a car manufacturer must endeavor to make a passenger car which meets these requirements. But it is a very difficult task. Incidentally, true quality characteristics must always be expressed in a language which consumers can understand.

A number of questions must be answered in determining true quality characteristics. These questions include the following: What do we mean by the term "easy driving"? How can we measure it? How can it be replaced by numerical values? What structure is to be used for the passenger car? In what way do tolerances in each part of a car affect its operation? How can we determine tolerances? What raw materials are to be used? How can we determine the prices of raw materials?

It is not easy to be a manufacturer. Japanese products now receive accolades for having the best quality in the world. This is made possible by the manufacturers' continuous attention to these various questions and to their effort in quality analysis.

In summary, the following three steps must be followed. They are very important in QC implementation:

1. Understand true quality characteristics.
2. Determine methods of measuring and testing true quality characteristics. This task is so difficult that, in the end, the five senses (sensory test) may be used to make the determination.

3. Discover substitute quality characteristics, and have a correct understanding of the relationship betweeen true quality characteristics and substitute quality characteristics.

To make sure that all QC participants can understand these three steps, companies are encouraged to use actual (finished) products for study—investigating one's own product can accomplish a great deal. But product research is a very expensive process, and sometimes one company alone cannot handle the task. It may become necessary to have a joint testing conducted by the manufacturer and the consumers (users).

The above is called quality analysis or quality function deployment. A number of methods, systems, and statistical methods have been invented to do quality analysis. However, they are too specialized to be dealt with adequately in this volume.

How Do We Express Quality?

When true quality characteristics are determined, there still remains the question of what language to use in expressing them. Consumers' requirements cannot always be expressed in a form that is easy to implement by manufacturers. Varied interpretations are always possible. And when interpretations differ, methods of production can also become varied. Here are some pointers in expressing quality.

1. Determine the Assurance Unit.

A light bulb or a radio can be counted one by one, so we shall call it a product unit. It becomes an assurance unit at the same time in that a consumer's main concern is the quality of each usable unit. So far so good, but what can be done when a product cannot be classified by product unit? The examples are many, from electric wire, thread, paper, ingredients or components or constituent parts which form together in chemical products, ore, and oil, to those products which are in powder or liquid form. It is difficult to define a unit in the examples listed.

Let me cite from my own experience the case of assigning an assurance unit to fertilizer. Ammonium sulphate is a type of fertilizer which requires a purity of 21 percent. What does this 21 percent mean? It can be interpreted as part of the daily amount produced. Thus if one thousand tons are produced in a day, and if the average purity for that 1,000 tons is more than 21 percent, that will suffice. Or one may get the mean value of more than 21 percent for a bag, or for each crystal. In the first instance the assurance unit is 1,000 tons, while in the last the assurance unit is each crystal.

Unless the assurance unit is made clear, even if one wishes to give quality assurance, such a guarantee cannot be given for sure. In the case under discussion, government bureaus and fertilizer manufacturers got together and determined one bag (that is 37.5 kg.) as the assurance unit, taking into account the convenience of farmers who are the customers.

2. Determine the Measuring Method.

When one wishes to give an exact definition of quality, if the method of measurement is vague, then nothing can be accomplished. However, true quality characteristics are very difficult to measure. Previously we spoke of one of the true quality characteristics of newsprint rolls to be "not tearing while being printed on by a rotary press." But how can the characteristic be measured? Rotary presses differ from one newspaper company to another. As for automobiles, how can one measure the characteristic of being "easy driving"?

Some characteristics can be measured physically or chemically, while others may have to depend on five human sense perceptions (the sensory test), color, sound, smell, taste, and touch.

In quality competition, the industry which has learned to measure these characteristics will emerge a winner.

3. Determine the Relative Importance of Quality Characteristics.

Seldom does a product have only one quality characteristic. Normally it has many characteristics. Take the example of newsprint rolls. In addition to the quality characteristic of "not tearing while being printed on by a rotary press," there can be other characteristics such as "ink does not penetrate to the other side," and "it prints clearly."

One must clearly differentiate the relative importance of the many quality characteristics that a product possesses. Generally, I cite defects and flaws and classify them as follows:

A critical defect—the quality characteristic which relates to life and safety. For example, tires that come off a car or brakes that do not function.

A major defect—the quality characteristic which seriously affects the proper functioning of a product. For example, the engine of a car does not work.

A minor defect—the quality characteristic which does not affect the proper functioning of a product, but is not appreciated by customers. For example, a scratch mark on a car.

For some products, categorization in greater detail may be necessary. Generally speaking one can never allow a critical defect, but a small number of minor defects is acceptable.

Assigning relative importance, or in other words, creating a priority orientation, is an important concept in the implementation of QC.

Defects and flaws in quality, as discussed above, are called *backward-looking quality*. In contrast, "good acceleration" and "easy driving" are characteristics which can become a product's sales points. They are called *forward-looking quality*. Unless emphasis is placed on this forward-looking quality, and sales points are made clear, the product cannot be sold.

People often consider all points equally important, but the inability to assign relative importance will result in creating mediocre products.

4. Arrive at a Consensus on Defects and Flaws.

People think differently about defects and flaws. This is true with manufacturers and consumers as well as among people within the same company.

This human tendency is often discernible when the five senses are utilized to make inspection (the sensory test). Some people will consider a scratch on a painted surface a flaw, but other people will say that since it does not affect the operation of a car, it cannot be considered a flaw. With regard to the tonal quality of a radio, differences in opinion often cannot be reconciled. The limits to defects and flaws in these instances are difficult to put in writing, and to formalize them into industrial standards is a very cumbersome and forbidding task. The best solution for this type of problem is for manufacturers and consumers to enter into full consultation and determine sets of allowable limits for future reference.

Let me cite an extreme case. Before visiting a machine works, I asked each workshop to make a histogram concerning its quality control. The graph on page 52 (Diagram III-2) was one of them.

I entered tolerance limits on the graph as indicated by the dotted lines. From that graph, it appeared that about one-half of the machine works' products was defective. So I asked the inspection division to find the defect rate, which came to only 0.3 percent. I asked if they made adjustments or reworked those pieces which were outside the tolerance limits before shipment. The answer was in the negative. This was rather strange, and we probed further into the case. What became clear was that there were separate inspection standards with a much wider degree of tolerances than the tolerance limits indicated. A given

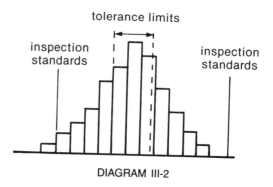

DIAGRAM III-2

piece falling within these inspection standards had been used by the next process without complaint. In fact the inspection standards were adopted to reflect this existing practice.

In this factory there was no consensus among the different divisions concerning what would constitute defects. They could not determine if those products that were outside the tolerance limits were to be considered defective, or only those which did not meet the inspection standards.

In another case, an electrical manufacturing company claimed that parts defects came to 0.3 percent. But when I visited their assembly factory, the fact did not bear out this claim, so I engaged in the following survey. First, I selected at random samples of 100 kinds of parts, and then compared each of these parts against specifications found in blueprints. For each blueprint, I could find on the average three discrepancies. This meant that the percent defective would have amounted to 300 percent. I also discovered that if products were assembled with parts manufactured in accordance with these blueprints, the task of assembly would be very difficult.

Actually there were also problems with the blueprints. But no blueprint had ever been revised, and shops continued production by changing the measurements of each item. The factory did ask the design division to revise blueprints, but the inflexible designers were too proud to make the revisions. In terms of product fidelity to the blueprints, every piece became by definition defective. But if workers made parts in accordance with the blueprints, defects became a reality. Theoretically they had to be guided by the blueprints, but in practice they treated these parts as special acceptance pieces to circumvent specifications found in the blueprints. Despite this compromise, many of the parts remained difficult to assemble.

This is another good example of the lack of consensus in a company. Unfortunately this example is not uncommon. Machine and electrical machine manufacturers would do well to check their parts manufacturing against their blueprints.

5. Expose Latent Defectives.

As is clear from the above examples, figures for defectives in factories and industries are merely the tip of the iceberg, yet they are called actual defectives. If we consider "defectives" in a broader sense, there may be ten or one hundred times more actual defectives than are discovered. To expose these hidden defectives, or latent defectives, is a basic goal of QC.

Some people consider goods to be defective only when they cannot be used and have to be discarded. But we must think about this practice more carefully. Reworked goods, specially accepted goods, and adjusted goods are all defectives. Reworked goods are those which have to be modified because initially they did not meet the standards. Extra labor is needed to make them into acceptable products. So they must be classified as defectives. The term "specially accepted goods" is a euphemism. It refers to those goods for which standards are lowered in order to meet the date of delivery. One has to pretend that they are not substandard. But, of course, they are also defectives.

In the assembly process, if a product such as a camera or a radio can be assembled and shipped without going through adjustment or rework, it is considered a good product. If it has to be adjusted or reworked in the assembly process, even if the end product is good, it still remains a defective product. In assembly, a good product is created when it goes straight from the first process to the end without adjustment or modification. We shall call the rate of its becoming a good product in this fashion the *go-straight-percentage*. Those products that do not go through the process straight from beginning to end tend to become damage prone after reaching the hands of consumers. Companies must strive to control design and process in such a way as to attain a go-straight-percentage of 95 to 100 percent.

If we observe the matter carefully and critically, we can find many latent defectives and latent workload associated with defective processes in our industries. When we begin QC we must immediately establish a clear definition of defects and expose and eliminate those latent defectives and the latent workload associated with defective processes.

6. Observe Quality Statistically.

When we examine products and work processes around us, we discover that no two are identical. We can always find differences.

If we study any one product, we find that many factors influence its production, including raw material, equipment, work method, and worker. It is impossible to make another one exactly like it. Quality of product always varies widely. In other words, if we view quality of product as a whole, it demonstrates a statistical distribution.

Quality for each individual item is of course important. But in practice we deal with quality in groups of so many dozens or so many hundred pieces. Take the example of a light bulb; singly its life may vary widely from 100 hours to 2,000 hours, or in a group of bulbs the dispersion may be within the range of 900 hours to 1,100 hours. Consumers will prefer the latter where dispersion is smaller and quality is more uniform and stable.

When we think of quality, we must consider its statistical distribution within groups and then proceed to implement process control and engage in inspection. To express a distribution, the mean value and a standard deviation will be used, but a more detailed treatment of this subject must be left for another book.

7. "Quality of Design" and "Quality of Conformance"

Quality of design is often called targeted quality. An industry wishes to create a product with a certain level of quality—hence targeted quality. Take the example of the light bulb just discussed. The manufacturer can aim for a light bulb with a life of 900 to 1,100 hours, or one with a life of 2,000 to 2,500 hours. Generally, if one wishes to raise quality of design the cost also rises.

Quality of conformance is also called compatible quality in that it is an indication of how far the actual products conform to quality of design. If there is a discrepancy between quality of design and quality of conformance, it means that there are defects or reworks. When quality of conformance goes up, cost comes down.

People who are not familiar with quality control say that if QC is implemented, cost will rise and productivity will fall. If one equates inspection with QC, cost indeed will rise, especially if one relies on the old style of QC which places emphasis on inspection. It is also true that if one raises quality of design, cost will rise accordingly. However, when quality of conformance improves, incidences of defects, reworks, and adjustments decline, resulting in cost decrease and productivity gain. Furthermore, if quality of design matches consumer requirements, sales will increase, creating an economy of scale. This leads to rationalization, and cost will come down even further. Japanese products have become highly competitive in the world market. This success has been the result of multiplier effects of the qualities of design and conformance.

In order to win in international competition, Japan has raised its quality of design continuously. Cost has, of course, gone up with it. By applying process control effectively, however, quality of conformance has improved. Lower incidence of defects and reworks, or even their elimination, have resulted in a cost down. Japan's targeted quality has met with the approval of consumers, and its products have sold very well. The result has been a reduction in cost, and quality products have been manufactured inexpensively.

Control of Quality Standards

There are no standards—whether they be national, international or company-wide—that are perfect. Usually standards contain some inherent defects. Consumer requirements also change continuously, demanding higher quality year after year. Standards that were adequate when they were first established, quickly become obsolete.

We engage in QC to satisfy consumer requirements. We emphasize that "In implementing quality control, do not seek merely to fulfill national standards and company standards, but set your goals to meet the quality requirements of consumers."

In practice, we must continuously review our own quality standards, revise them, and improve them.

What Dr. Deming emphasized in his 1950 seminar was precisely this point. As Diagram III-3 shows, he spoke of a cycle of design, production, sales, and market research, which is to be followed by another cycle that begins with redesigning based on the experience obtained in the previous cycle. In this manner, redesigning of quality occurs continuously and quality will improve continuously. What this approach suggests is that the manufacturer must always be keenly attentive to consumer requirements, and the opinions of consumers must be anticipated as the manufacturer establishes his own standards. Unless this is done, QC cannot achieve its goals, nor can it assure quality to consumers.

We do not think of consumers merely as people who buy things. When we look at a product or a work process we realize that it has been created or accomplished through the cooperation of many people. Work comes to one person from the person ahead of him or from the

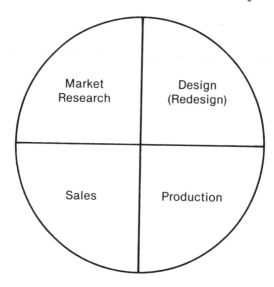

Deming's Quality Cycle

DIAGRAM III-3

preceding process, and his task is to add his work and then transmit it to the person following him. This is the way we work. We follow the saying that "the next process is our customer." Indeed the next process is a consumer and a customer.

Good control means allowing quality standards to be revised constantly to reflect the voices of consumers and their complaints as well as the requirements of the next process. Standards are by nature fixed in that they must achieve standardization and uniformity. But one cannot allow fixity to go too far. Excessive adherence to standards can lead to arrogance within the industry, coercion by the state, and unhappiness for consumers.

My slogan is this: "If standards and regulations are not revised in six months, it is proof that no one is seriously using them."

III. HOW TO LOOK AT CONTROL

When we first started our QC activities in Japan, the most difficult task was dealing with the concept behind the term control (*kanri*). We had to devise a way to let all employees—from top executives down to middle management, engineers, and workers—understand the meaning of "control" and let them implement it.

Another difficulty we had to face was the plethora of words available to describe the concept in Japan as well as in other countries. In Japanese the words *keiei, kanri, kansei,* and *tōsei* are all similar in meaning. In English there are words like management, control, and administration. Depending on the country from which one comes, or who one is, the word "control" assumes a different meaning. If we try to pursue this subject further, there will be no limit to our discussion. In the end, word choice becomes a matter of personal taste, so to save time we will suspend this discussion.

The words "management," "control," and "administration" do have differing nuances. But they also have a common denominator. Each of these words implies that one must set a goal or target and find a way to realize it efficiently.

Academic subjects such as physics, chemistry, and mathematics are universal and are common to all nations, political systems, races, and religions. However, when one comes to the matter of control or management, human factors must be taken into account, and it cannot be common to all nations.

Japan's QC originally came from the West. If it had been adopted without modification, it would not have succeeded. We have sprinkled this QC with Japanese seasoning and made it more palatable to the Japanese taste. A lot of thought has gone into it to make it a Japanese-style QC. I have discussed QC's transformation in Chapter 2 but left the questions of control and its implementation unanswered. So I shall now proceed with these two topics.

Problems of Control in the Past

The concepts of control and organization were introduced to Japan long before the Second World War. They were adopted and practiced by Japanese industries. Of course, there were many problems associated with them.

"Don't produce defective products," "lower the cost," and "be efficient," were among the commands given by top executives in olden days. Actually, in those days giving commands such as these seemed to be the only task executives performed.

These commands passed through the channel from the president to directors, from directors to factory managers, from factory managers to section chiefs, from section chiefs to foremen, and from foremen to line workers. I said "through the channel," but it was more like a tunnel. When commands went through the tunnel smoothly they performed some useful functions. But more often than not, many of these commands simply got stuck in the middle and were distorted, and some never reached the line workers for whom they were intended. The president might command, "Do not ship defective products," and the foreman at the shipping department might translate it to read as follows: "Let us meet the delivery date by sending these defective products; they aren't that bad."

Top executives in those days would command their subordinates to do their best or work harder. I call this type of control a form of "spiritualism," appealing to the so-called "Japanese spirit," and calling for chores to be performed without the carrot sticks. As long as people are people, spirituality is important, but man cannot survive by "spirit" alone. No effective and lasting control could emerge through this approach.

When a manufacturing plant produces defective products or otherwise fails, only one-fourth or one-fifth of the fault can be assigned to line workers. Most of the fault is attributable to executives, managers or staff. The "spiritual" system of control simply tries to shift the blame to those who are at the bottom.

There were other problems when we began QC in Japan. They were:

1. Too many abstract theories of control, which were not practical. There was no scientific and rational methodology.
2. There was no full participation when examination of the means to reach the goals was conducted.
3. Participants were not familiar with analysis and control techniques based on statistical methods.
4. Education on quality and control was not given to all employees from the president down.
5. There were few specialists, but they only thought in terms of their own specialization and did not see the overall picture.
6. Top executives and middle managers set policies that were often of the spur-of-the-moment variety. They also issued commands which were contradictory.
7. There was prevalence of sectionalism. Divisions engaged in in-fighting and refused to assume responsibilities.

The above may sound familiar to readers, because these problems may characterize today's business world as well, but I shall leave the comparison to the reader's own judgment.

How to Proceed with Control

What steps can one take? If I were to describe the entire control procedure, there would simply be not enough pages in this book. So I shall attempt to present a bare outline.

Dr. Taylor used to describe control with these words, "plan—do—see." What does the word "see" mean? To Japanese middle school students, it simply means to look at, and that does not convey Taylor's meaning. So we have rephrased it as follows: "plan—do—check—action" (PDCA). This is what we call the Control Circle, Diagram III-4, and it must be made to move in the right direction. I have found it advisable to redefine this circle by dividing it into six categories. Control is to be organized based on these six categories, which have proven successful.

The six steps are as follows:

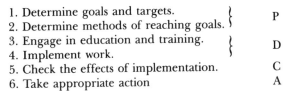

1. Determine goals and targets. } P
2. Determine methods of reaching goals. }
3. Engage in education and training. } D
4. Implement work. }
5. Check the effects of implementation. C
6. Take appropriate action A

Control Circle

DIAGRAM III-4

I shall now explain important issues connected with each of these steps.

1. Determine Goals and Targets—These Can Be Determined by Policies—Are the Bases for Determining the Policies Clear? Are Data Clear?

Unless policies are determined, no goals can be established. These policies must be determined by the top management. This does not mean that directors of divisions or section chiefs cannot have policies. Anyone who has the term "chief" or its equivalent on his title must have his own policy. To parrot the policy given by a superior and give it to a subordinate is an archaic method of transmission that is much like giving a command through a tunnel.

If one is to issue a policy statement, the basis for arriving at that policy and the data supporting it must be made clear. The chief executive officer is the one who determines top policies, but it is his or her subordinates and staff who must supply the rationale for the policies, assemble supporting data, and analyze them. In order not to be unduly influenced by off-the-cuff remarks of the president, the staff must assemble data and analyze them carefully at all times. When division directors or section chiefs determine their policies, similar processes must be carried out by their staff assistants. A common weakness in Japanese industry has been that when top executives and middle managers make their policies, they often lack rationale, data, and information, or even when they do have these, they fail to analyze them adequately.

Because of this lack of data, it normally takes several years before policy control or goal control—that is, management by objectives—can take hold.

In making a policy, an executive must always keep an overall picture in mind. It is understandable to issue a policy stating that "defects must be decreased" when defects come to 30 to 40 percent. But suppose the same executive also issues a policy stating "maintain the production quota." Line workers will be perplexed. For this reason, when determining policies and goals, confine them to priority items only. Ideally there should not be more than three, or if necessary five, such priority items, but five should be the absolute upper limit.

Once a policy is determined, goals will become self-evident. These goals must be expressed concretely in figures. To do so, you need a rationale as the basis. Goals must also be expressed purposefully. Demonstrate the goals to the employees, using concrete terms and figures; tell them everything they need to know, including information about personnel, quality, cost, profit, amount of production, and date of delivery. Don't give abstract commands like "study" or "control effectively." These terms may sound good methodologically, but cannot result in good control practices.

In setting up goals, a clear-cut deadline must be assigned. It is also necessary to determine the upper and lower limits of attainable goals. For example, there should be some goals which must be reached at all costs, and there should be other goals which one endeavors to reach.

Goals are to be set on the basis of problems the company wishes to solve. It is far better to do it this way than to assign separate goals for different divisions and organizations. Goals must be established in such a way as to insure cooperation by all divisions.

Policies and goals must be put in writing and widely distributed. The lower the level of the employees that policies and goals reach in the organizational chart, the better they must be in the amount of information provided and in the degree of explicitness and concreteness. At the same time, all policy and goal statements must be consistent. (This process is called policy deployment and goal deployment.)

From the perspective of management, goals can be divided into priority goals and routine goals. In other words, control must also be divided into priority control and routine control. Once policies for a given fiscal year are determined, the fiscal year plan and fiscal year goals will automatically follow. Concurrently, priority goals and routine goals will also be established.

I am not happy with the terms *policy control* and *goal control.* Fundamentally no control can exist where policies and goals are absent. Thus it is redundant to use words such as "policy" and "goal" to modify the word "control." I object to these terms on another ground; if one is to over-emphasize policies and goals, they are likely to be misused in the fashion of "Japanese spirit" control, with managers insisting that their subordinates work harder without giving them the requisite tools to do so.

Of course, it sounds good to say "policy control" and "goal control," so I shall compromise. But please be sure to have an understanding of the concepts underlying the term "control" as I have outlined. Without that understanding, QC activities cannot succeed.

2. Determine Methods of Reaching the Goals—Standardizing Your Work.

If goals and targets are established without being accompanied by the methods to reach them, QC will end up in mere mental exercise.

One can set a goal of reducing the defect rate to below three percent, but one cannot simply pat people on the back and say, "work hard, work hard." That would be no different from the Japanese militarist who ordered everyone to shoot down American bombers with bamboo spears during the Second World War. Unless one establishes scientific and rational methods of reaching the goals, nothing can be accomplished.

Yet there are many varieties of methods. An individual may choose to do things his own idiosyncratic way, and it may prove to be the best method for him. But an organization cannot rely on a method thus derived. Even if it were a superior technique, it would still remain the specialty of one individual and could not be adopted as the technology of the company or workplace.

Here I am going to state that determining a method equals standardization. This may at first sound strange. But what I mean is this: if a person determines a method, he must standardize it and make it into a regulation, and then incorporate it into the company's technology and property. What I am suggesting is that the method to be established must be useful to everyone and free of difficulty. It has to be standardized for that reason.

I have said that one should standardize and make regulations, but some pitfalls come to mind that must be avoided at all costs.

A. Detailed standards and regulations are useless if they are established by headquarters staff and engineer-specialists who do not know or do not try to know the workplace and who ignore the wishes of the people who have to use them. It is not uncommon to find headquarters staff and technicians who enjoy making things uncomfortable for the workplace by creating cumbersome standards and regulations. If we find many national standards unsatisfactory, a possible inference is that they may also have been established under conditions similar to that just described.

B. In this world some people are born regulators. They love to make as many regulations as possible to bind other people, and consider that to be good management. Regulations for what? It is hard to understand. When they are not consistent with commonly held goals, standardizations and regulations only make work more difficult. They hinder efficiency and ignore humanity.

The two statements above point out the danger of over-standardization and over-regulation. Now I would like to summarize my own thoughts.

In Diagram III-5, the effect is found at the right-hand end. Achieving quality characteristics is the effect and is also the goal of the system. The words appearing on the tips of the branches are causes. In QC the causes given in this illustration are called cause factors.

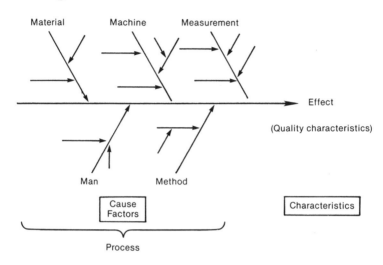

Cause and Effect Diagram

DIAGRAM III-5

We call a collection of these cause factors a process. Process does not refer merely to the manufacturing process. Work relating to design, purchasing, sales, personnel, and administration are all processes. Politics, government, and education are all processes. As long as there are causes and effects, or cause factors and characteristics, they can all be processes. In QC we believe that process control can be beneficial to all of these processes.

Lately there has been a boom of a sort in total quality control (TQC) activities, and TQC is spreading to hotels, department stores, banks, and construction industries, which are different from traditional manufacturing industries. There is nothing strange about this new phenomenon. My feeling is that people are finally beginning to understand the true value of QC.

Our belief is that the process, which is a collection of cause factors, must be controlled to obtain better products and effects. This approach anticipates problems and prevents them before they actually occur, so we shall call it vanguard control. In contrast, if a person worries about the performance of his company only after the fact—for example, finding that sales do not meet the quota near the end of each month and quickly trying to force sales—that method is called rear guard control.

The diagram above shows the relationship between characteristics and cause factors, so I have named it the cause and effect diagram. In QC one cannot simply present a goal and shout "work hard, work hard." One must understand the meaning of process control, take hold of the process, which is a collection of cause factors, and build within that process ways of making better products, establishing better goals, and achieving effects. To facilitate that thought process I invented the diagram. In 1952 all processes in the Kawasaki Iron Fukiai Works adopted this diagram to effect standardization and control. The results were gratifying, and the diagram has since been adopted in many workplaces all over the world. Dr. Juran has honored me in his 1962 *QC Handbook* by calling the cause and effect diagram the Ishikawa Diagram, and it is now known by that name. The diagram's shape has also given it a nickname, the Fishbone Diagram.

The number of cause factors is infinite. Whatever work and whatever process one picks, one can immediately identify ten or twenty cause factors. If one would wish to control all of these cause factors, the task would prove impossible. Even if it were possible, it would be highly uneconomical.

While there are many cause factors, the truly important ones, the cause factors which will sharply influence effects, are not many. If we follow the principle set by Vilfredo Pareto, all we have to do is standardize two or three of the most important cause factors and control them. But first these important cause factors must be found.

In searching for these important cause factors, people who are familiar with a particular process, such as workers, engineers, and researchers, must all be consulted. They must be able to discuss the process openly and frankly, and the session can be conducted as a brainstorming session. The opinions presented in this session must be analyzed statistically and must be checked scientifically and rationally against the data available. (This is called process analysis.) A conclusion thus obtained can be understood and accepted by all. This is the first step toward standardization. Lately the task of establishing or revising standards has been done by QC circles because of their intimate knowledge of the workplace.

My view is that the task of establishing standardization or setting up regulations should be done in order to delegate authority to subordinates. The key to success is to standardize aggressively those things which are plainly understandable and to let a subordinate handle them.

One thing that must be kept in mind is how to handle an emergency. The following must be made clear:

- Who is to do what in an emergency? How far does any person's authority extend?
- From whom does a person get instructions?

I have spoken about this before, but I must reemphasize. Standards and regulations are imperfect. They must be reviewed and revised constantly. "If newly established standards and regulations are not revised in six months, it is proof that no one is seriously using them." When people engage in process analysis and revise standards, technology will advance and accumulate within the industry.

3. Engage in Education and Training.

Superiors have the responsibility of educating and nurturing their subordinates.

Work standards and technical standards can be made into superb regulations, but when they are distributed employees may not read them. Or when they read them they may not understand the thought process behind the regulations or the way they must be handled. The important thing is to educate the people who are going to be affected by these standards and regulations.

Education is not confined to the norm of formal meetings. Assembling people in a classroom and giving them lectures can be at best only one-third or one-fourth of the total educational process. A superior must educate his subordinate on a one-to-one basis through actual work. Once the subordinate is educated in this manner, delegate authority to him and let him have the freedom to do his job. In this way the subordinate will grow.

I am an advocate of quality control based on belief in people's goodness. If a person does not trust his allotted number of subordinates and imposes strict control and frequent inspection, he cannot be a good manager. His control is based on the belief that people are by nature evil, and such a system simply does not work. An ideal form of management creates a situation in which everyone is well-trained, can be trusted, and need not be supervised excessively.

Man is by nature good. If educated he can become a reliable person to whom authority can be delegated. That is why I stress education. Through education and training subordinates become reliable, and the span of control (the number of people one person can supervise directly) becomes larger and larger. My ideal is to have one supervisor for every one hundred workers, just like an orchestra where the conductor can bring out the best in music!

4. Implement Work.

If everything is done according to the procedure explained above, implementation should pose no problem. But let us think about this for a moment.

One can force subordinates to implement work by giving a command, but that will never go over smoothly. Conditions change constantly, and the commands given by superiors can never catch up with changing conditions. I stress voluntarism in QC for this very reason.

There are many reasons for the failure of America's Zero Defect Movement, one being that the movement was made into a mere mental exercise that used people as machines and disregarded the fact that people are people. Another reason for its failure comes from the view that if standards are strictly adhered to, the number of defects will equal zero. I will repeat once more. Standards and regulations are always inadequate. Even if they are strictly followed, defects and flaws will appear. It is experience and skill that make up for inadequacies in standards and regulations.

Please note that problems related to implementation appear at every step of management and control.

5. Check the Effects of Implementation.

How can one check whether or not the work is being implemented smoothly?

To give a command, to give a direction, or to give training is not sufficient in discharging one's responsibility as the top executive, as a manager, or as a staff member. Up to now, there have been too many instances of management giving commands and directions without adequate checking.

If one is to proceed and say "check this and check that" constantly, it will never succeed, because it is a form of management based on the assumption that man is by nature evil. But management cannot be management if there is no system of checking at all. Laissez-faire does not make a person a manager. Ideally, things ought to proceed without a hitch without checking, but that does not happen. Yet in my experience, the act of checking has been for all practical purposes and intents neglected, and that is the reason that I have to stress its importance here.

In management the most important concern is the exception principle. If things are progressing according to the goals set and according to the standards, then let things be as they are. But when unusual events occur, or matters are anything but routine, then the manager must step in. The purpose of checking is to discover these exceptions. In order to perform that task efficiently, the basic policies, goals, and standardization and education procedures must all be clearly understood. Unless these are clearly stated, and unless there are reliable standards, one cannot tell which are exceptions and which are not. Some top managers insist on checking without announcing their policies and goals. I call this strategy "A flying crow always catches something." It is unfair to their subordinates, who do not know on what basis they are being checked.

Now how does one go about finding exceptions?

A. Check the causes.

The first step in checking is to see if all cause factors are under control. In other words, you must check each process, such as design, purchasing, and manufacturing, to see if cause factors are clearly understood in accordance with the standards set. You must check those cause factors identified in the cause and effect diagram.

To do so, you need to visit each of the workplaces. Indeed, it is a time-honored adage that the workplace must be visited. It is not good just to walk over there. Have a definite purpose in mind, and check what you can see, always comparing it against the standards and regulations. The number of the cause factors involved is limitless and cannot be checked by one person, so priority must be given to those cause factors that are more important, or that if left alone may be dangerous. A checklist will be helpful. Often inadequacies in work standards can also be discovered during the check. We call the cause factors which must be checked the "check items."

The task of checking cause factors must be given to lower-level managers. There are some people who love to engage in the task of checking cause factors in detail, even though they have attained the positions of division heads or company directors. But people who are placed in these positions should check the effects from a higher and wider perspective. They must not be saddled with the task of checking these cause factors. People who do that are essentially performing the function of a foreman, so I call them *division foremen* and *director foremen*.

B. Check through the effects.

Another method is to check a process or work by its effects, in other words, to check characteristics as shown in the cause and effect diagram. Among the effects are matters relating to personnel (rate of attendance, number of proposals presented, etc.); quality; quantity; date of delivery; amount of material, labor, and mechanical power required for production of a product unit; and cost. By observing changes taking place in each of these items, one can check the process, work, and management.

If effects are found wanting, it means that something unusual is happening in some of the processes and there are problems there. A manager's function is to discover the reasons for the irregularity, which lie in the cause factors. As long as a manager has a handle on these cause factors, controlling the process will present no problem.

There are certain items that are called *control items.* They are items used to check processes and management through their effects. People who have subordinates under them must have control items. A foreman may have between five to twenty such items. Those who are section chiefs and above, including the president, normally have twenty to fifty control items.

Here I must caution the reader to check *by* or *through* the effects, and not *to* check the effects themselves. Let me illustrate this point by using quality as an example. We check process and management *through* quality. To check quality (effects) becomes an act of inspection that is completely separate from the notion of control. We examine quality to check the way process and management operate. We want to control process well in order to bring forth good products which flow through the process smoothly. The same can be said about cost control or other types of control; we control through cost, but we do not control cost.

Incidentally, effects vary widely. Even when the same person uses the same materials, the same equipment, and the same method to produce something, effects will still vary. People may think that under a uniform process, uniform effects will occur, but they are wrong. As long as we have people who follow this pattern of thinking, we can never be free of false data from industries and workplaces.

In QC, effects are recorded sequentially on a graph on which statistically secured control limits are noted. Through this graph we attempt to discover exceptions. Cause factors are limitless. Thus effects, such as quality, or the amount of production and cost, will all vary widely. In other words, effects have a distribution. We use this statistical concept "distribution" to discover exceptions (irregularity). The tool we use in checking distribution is called a control chart.

If we are to find unusual cause factors in process and management through effects, we have to make sure that the past records of the lot and other data are available. Which materials and which parts did this product use? Who used which equipment to produce it and when did this occur? In other words, stratification in the lot must be tightly constructed. Stratification is the most important concept in QC. Without a tightly constructed stratification no analysis or control will be possible.

The effects obtained through this check must be fed back to the divisions and workers concerned. This must be done as soon as possible. Reasons for exceptions may be found, and their cause factors can then be dealt with promptly.

6. Take Appropriate Action.

Checking through effects to find exceptions or something unusual does not in itself serve the interests of the company. The cause factors for these exceptions must be found and appropriate actions taken.

In taking corrective action, it is important to take measures to prevent recurrence of these exceptions. One must put brakes on the irregularities. In any instance, making adjustments to the cause factors involved will not be enough; one must endeavor to remove the cause factors which have been responsible for the exceptions. Adjustment and prevention of recurrence are two separate things, both conceptually and in terms of the actions to be taken. In removing the causes for exceptions, one must go back to the very source of the problem to take measures to prevent recurrence. It is simple to say "prevent recurrence," but such prevention is very difficult to practice. More often than not, temporary measures are applied to patch up problems for the time being. Prevention of recurrence is such an important concept in QC that I must return to it in the next chapter.

The above is an outline of what control is all about. If you wish to know why control is not carried out effectively, reread the factors described in steps 1 through 6. Most of the reasons can be inferred from them.

I suggest that you follow these steps faithfully, and take a new look at your own place of work.

Now here are some words of caution, based on my own experiences and observations:

A. Don't be angry with your subordinates when they make mistakes. They are usually responsible for one-fourth or one-fifth of these mistakes. By getting angry, you make truth disappear. Subordinates become more prone to provide you with false data and reports. Create a mood in which your subordinates will feel free to report to their superiors and colleagues about their own mistakes. To prevent recurrence of mistakes, make sure that everyone is involved in discussing the problem.

B. If you often come up with the excuse, "I don't know," it is because your own thought on control lacks thoroughness. If control is thoroughly carried out, "I don't know" will disappear.

C. After you have taken an action, always check the effect. Then recheck that effect to see if you have been successful in preventing recurrence (of errors). You must go as far back as possible to the source of past problems. Even if you think you have taken the right action, you may still be mistaken. Checks must be carried out both for a short-range effect and for a long-range result.

D. Control does not mean maintenance of status quo. If you implement prevention of recurrence, little by little you will experience progress and advancement.

If statistical methods are used in the above six steps, the process becomes statistical control. With regard to quality it becomes statistical quality control, and with regard to cost it becomes statistical cost control.

Hindrance to Control and Improvement

There are several factors that hinder control and its resulting improvements. They usually stem from people, whose wrong attitudes are the main causes. I shall enumerate them below:

1. Passivity among top executives and managers; their avoidance of responsibility.

2. People who feel that everything is fine and that there are no problems at all. These are people who are satisfied with the status quo and lack in the understanding of significant issues.

3. People who think that their own company is by far the best. Let us call them egotists.

4. People who think that the easiest and best ways of doing things are those which are familiar to them. People who rely only on their own shallow experience.

5. People who think only of themselves or of their own division. People who are imbued with sectionalism.

6. People who have no ears for other people's opinions.

7. People who scramble for distinction, always thinking about themselves.

8. Despair, jealousy, and envy.

9: People who are oblivious to what is happening beyond their immediate surroundings. People who do not know anything about other divisions, other industries, the outside world, or the world as a whole.

10. People who continue to live in the feudalistic past. They include "people who are engaged merely in business affairs, managers and line workers who lack common sense, and labor union members who are doctrinaire."

To dispel these wrong attitudes, QC activists will need the courage of their conviction, the spirit of cooperation, an enthusiastic pioneering spirit, and the desire to make new breakthroughs. They also need confidence in their own ability to persevere and must possess good tactics and strategies for overcoming difficulties.

"When one wishes to implement something which is new, the greatest enemy of that effort can be found within one's own company and within one's self. Unless one can overcome this enemy, there can be no progress." I leave this chapter with a quote from that venerable cartoon character, Pogo: "We have met the enemy, and the enemy is us." Need I say more?

CHAPTER IV

Quality Assurance

Quality must be built into each design and each process. It cannot be created through inspection.

Quality control that emphasizes inspection is old-style QC.

The basic notion behind control is prevention of recurrence (of errors).

The very essence of TQC is in the quality control and quality assurance of new product development.

Remove the cause, the basic cause, and not the symptoms.

When all of a company's new products succeed and consumers say, "We can buy their new products gladly with confidence," then that company's QC has truly come of age.

I. QUALITY CONTROL AND QUALITY ASSURANCE

Quality assurance is the very essence of quality control.

Japanese companies have been guided by the principle of "quality first" in accepting and practicing total quality control. This principle has enabled Japanese industry to produce quality goods at low cost with high productivity, thus maintaining an edge in the export market. Japanese commodities of exceptional reliability—automobiles, cameras, color televisions, video recorders, and iron and steel products—are welcomed by consumers all over the world. Companies that have emphasized "quality first" have been able to upgrade quality phenomenally. Over a period of time, this has resulted in a substantial increase in productivity which has in turn made it possible to effect a cost down, which then has led to an increase in sales and in profit.

In contrast, American managers have taken the path of seeking short-range goals. They have adhered to the principle of "profit first" and in the process lost to Japan in competition. Lately, Western countries have become aware of this fact, and there is now a discernible trend in the press and in the academic circles toward suggesting that "the West must learn from Japan."

This chapter deals with the subject of management according to the principle of quality first, or that of quality assurance, which constitutes the very essence of total quality control.

There are three important considerations to take into account when dealing with quality assurance.

1. A company must assure quality which meets the requirements of consumers (true quality characteristics). The issue is not one of meeting national standards. Of course, a company will have no right to discuss quality assurance if its products do not even meet national standards.

2. A similar concern must be expressed in the case of exporting to foreign countries. All products shipped abroad must meet the requirements of consumers abroad.

A large number of automobiles has been shipped to the United States, creating an imbalance in the two countries' trade and the so-called trade friction.

Why do Japanese cars sell well in the United States? The answer is very simple. Japanese manufacturers have been able to produce cars that meet the requirements of American consumers and to assure quality for those cars. Japanese manufacturers make cars with steering wheels on the left for export to the United States (as compared to domestic cars which have steering wheels on the right. In Japan, traffic moves on the left-hand side.) All of these cars are economical to maintain, are defect-free, and have excellent gas mileage. In contrast, American manufacturers do not produce cars that meet the requirements of Japanese consumers. Their fuel consumption is high, and they break down frequently. The cost of maintenance is high. U.S. companies ignore Japan's traffic pattern and retain the steering wheel on the left. Some do place the steering wheel on the right, but have not made adjustments for it to function properly in that position. No wonder that, except for a few who are interested in owning foreign cars for foreign cars' sake, no one really wants to buy American-made cars in Japan.

3. Top executives must recognize the importance of quality assurance and make sure that the entire company will give its utmost to this common goal. By proceeding effectively with quality assurance, the company (a) can bring happiness and satisfaction to customers all over the world, which in turn will contribute to its sales figures, and (b) can in the long-run earn good profits, which will satisfy executives, employees, and shareholders.

II. WHAT IS QUALITY ASSURANCE?

In short, quality assurance means to assure quality in a product so that a customer can buy it with confidence and use it for a long period of time with confidence and satisfaction.

To be able to buy with confidence a customer must have a sense of trust in a particular product from a particular company that has a record of having shipped reliable products for a long period of time. This kind of trust cannot be built overnight and can only be obtained through the company's long-term efforts for quality assurance. "It takes ten years to build confidence in your products, but that confidence can be lost overnight." This point must be fully recognized by everyone who deals with products.

Our next point is customer satisfaction. Of course, the product sold must not be flawed or defective, but this alone is not sufficient. It is necessary to insure quality of design, making certain that the product is fully functional in the way the consumer expects. In other words, the product must have true quality characteristics. Quality assurance is almost like a contract entered into by the producer and his customer. In this producer–customer "contract," the way the product is being advertised must be taken into consideration. Exaggerated claims are not desirable. Entries in the catalogue, the contents of the brochure, the way sales personnel handle the product and explain it to customers, and the language they select all have a bearing on customer satisfaction.

When a customer expects to be able to use a product for a long period of time it means that the product must be sold under the premise of having the necessary durability. If it should break down unexpectedly, however, parts should be supplied expeditiously anywhere in the world. Technically competent and efficient after-service is always a must. I hope companies will adopt the policy that "as long as our products are being used, we will supply parts." It is not good to stop supplying parts five or ten years after production of the product has been terminated.

In order to provide true quality assurance, top executives must establish firm policies that will encompass all of the following divisions: research, planning, design, manufacturing, sales, and service. These policies must also reach subcontractors who supply parts to the company and reach the company's various distribution systems. Full quality assurance cannot be effected unless everyone is involved, including all employees, subcontractors, and distributors. Toyota Motors has a good movement that follows the slogan, "Quality is assured by all of us in Toyota."

III. PRINCIPLES OF QUALITY ASSURANCE

The responsibility for quality assurance rests with the manufacturer. He must satisfy his customers with quality in his products. If a product is made through a cooperative effort, the supplier assumes responsibility for quality assurance.

Within a company the responsibility for quality assurance rests with the divisions of design and manufacturing, and not with the division of inspection. The latter merely inspects products from the standpoint of consumers and does not assume responsibility for quality assurance.

IV. PROGRESS IN QUALITY ASSURANCE METHODS

Historically, Japan's quality assurance moved along the following lines:

1. Inspection-oriented quality assurance
2. Process control-oriented quality assurance
3. Quality assurance with emphasis on new product development

Inspection-oriented Quality Assurance

Historically, quality assurance started with doing inspection well. As discussed earlier, this approach was abandoned at a relatively early period in Japan, but in the West many people still consider inspection equals quality assurance. I think this stems from their basic assumption that man is by nature evil. No one knows what the manufacturing division is up to, so it must be supervised very strictly. To accomplish this, the inspection division is made independent and its authority is enhanced. In short, the basic emphasis is on strengthening inspection in order to bring about quality assurance. In the West, therefore, the ratio of inspectors to line workers is very high. The ratio in Japan generally runs to about five percent, and in some companies it is only one percent, but in the West, a ratio of fifteen percent is not uncommon.

During the period when the primary emphasis was on inspection QC was conducted by the division of quality control or the division of inspection. This approach caused a number of problems that raised some interesting points.

The first is that inspectors are unnecessary personnel who reduce the overall productivity of a company. They are not making anything. Inspection is necessary because defects and defectives exist. If defects and defectives disappear, inspectors become unnecessary.

The second is that in postwar Japan QC has been promoted with the view that responsibility for quality assurance rests with the producers. Needless to say, this concept is for the benefit of consumers, but it has been further extended to subcontractors and cooperating manufacturers. Parts and materials subcontracted must have their quality assurance from suppliers (in this case producers). The purchasers (for example assemblers and users) inspect at the time of purchase only if there is doubt of the reliability of the suppliers. If the suppliers are reliable on the matter of quality, purchase can be made without inspection. This is the so-called assured purchasing system.

Now let us apply this concept within a company. The producer, that is, the manufacturing division, assumes responsibility for quality assurance, and the inspection division does not. The latter's function is to check products from the point of view of consumers or of company managers.

We follow the doctrine that man is by nature good and accordingly educate the manufacturing division well. The division, being duly educated and trained, will control its process itself and self-inspect its own products before sending them off to the next process. It assures quality.

This has been the basis of our approach in conducting quality control since the end of the Second World War.

The third point deals with the issue of information feedback from the inspection division to the manufacturing division. This process takes too much time, and the data provided do not stratify sufficiently by lot. It is not always easy for the manufacturing division to use those data in applying temporary measures or in preventing recurrence. Often such data are simply useless. In contrast, if the line worker who is responsible for a particular product is given the task of self-inspection, feedback is instantaneous and action can be taken immediately. The latter approach ensures a sharp reduction in the number of defectives.

The fourth point deals with the question of production speed. When the speed accelerates, workers cannot inspect. Thus automated inspection must be considered.

The fifth point concerns the application of the statistical sampling method. The method may designate an acceptable quality level (AQL; the lowest quality acceptable) at one percent or at 0.5 percent. This is unsatisfactory for companies that seek high quality, such as those seeking a defect rate of 0.01 percent or those seeking ppm (parts per million) control (at a defect rate of one one-millionth).

The sixth deals with those many items whose quality cannot be assured through inspection alone. The quality of many complicated assembled commodities and materials cannot be known until used. When a company seeks ppm control based on a destructibility test, a rigorous performance test, or a reliability test, inspection is often uneconomical and cannot necessarily assure quality by itself.

Lastly, it must be noted that defects can indeed be uncovered through inspection, without the end result measuring up to true quality assurance. When defects are found, the only action the manufacturer can take is that of making adjustments, reworking the product, or consigning it to scrap. In any event, productivity suffers and cost rises. In addition, products that have been adjusted or reworked are more likely to break down, which is exactly the opposite of quality assurance.

As long as there are defects, all items must in principle be inspected. This may take the form of shipment inspection before the' product reaches the hands of customers, or shipment inspection during the manufacturing process, or self-inspection, or inspection by the inspection division. Many developing countries ship their products without imposing adequate inspection, knowing full well that these shipments contain many defectives. Obviously they are still at the pre-quality control stage.

Process Control-oriented Quality Assurance

As discussed above, quality assurance that relies on inspection creates a number of problems. Because of its disadvantages we abandoned this approach in 1949, shortly after we began QC in Japan. In its place we adopted quality assurance that emphasized process control. We studied process capabilities and made certain that each and every one of our products met quality standards through control of the manufacturing process.

In QC we say that "Quality must be built into each process." This saying was born when we deliberated on the issues involved in quality assurance.

Once we adopted the approach which emphasized process control, we could no longer rely exclusively on the existing inspection and QC divisions to perform the task of quality assurance. Everyone had to be involved. This meant that in addition to the inspection division, the divisions of purchasing, production engineering, manufacturing, and marketing and all subcontractors had to work together in discharging their respective QC obligations. It also meant that employees from the top executive to line workers had to participate in QC. In other words, all divisions and employees had to be involved.

However, it became clear to us that there was a limit to process control, and we could not engage in quality assurance by means of process control alone. Process control could not deal with the following matters: usability of products in the hands of consumers under various conditions and different methods of use; misuse of products by consumers; quality assurance in an emergency; and problems of reliability in a broader sense. Problems could occur in the designing or development process which obviously could not be solved by the manufacturing or inspection division. And no matter how hard a division engaged in process control, if the selection of materials were wrong, nothing could be accomplished.

Therefore, while process control remains an important concern and must continue to be practiced, we have discovered that it is indispensable to have quality assurance which begins at the stage where new products are developed.

Quality Assurance with Emphasis on New Product Development

In the late 1950s Japan began quality assurance with emphasis on new product development. At each step of the way from planning for new products to after-service, evaluation was to be tightly conducted and quality assured. These steps included new product planning, design, trial manufacturing, testing, subcontracting, purchasing, preparation for production, design for mass production, trial manufacturing for mass production, manufacturing, marketing, after-service, and management during transition from initial production to normal production. Prior to entering the stage of manufacturing, quality analysis had to be adequately performed, including testing for reliability under various conditions. Quality assurance and reliability assurance were thus built into the entire process.

Out of this experience came the saying that "Quality must be built into each design and each process."

Today many Japanese products are considered to be of the highest quality in the world. This is made possible by the tight quality assurance programs instituted while the products are in the stages of development.

I consider quality assurance for new product development a very important concept for three reasons.

1. Unless quality assurance is done well during the stage of new product development, no adequate quality assurance can be effected.
2. If a company fails in new product development, that company can come to the brink of bankruptcy. New product development should be the most important concern of the company.
3. If quality assurance is conducted for new product development, all divisions in the company can realize quality control and quality

assurance. These divisions include the divisions of research, planning, design, test manufacturing, purchasing, subcontracting, production engineering, manufacturing, inspection, marketing, and after-service. QC learned in the head alone is practically useless. Theory and practice must work hand in hand from an early stage of new product development. As the Chinese say, "To know reality, one must seek and act upon it."

With these points in mind, whenever I am asked to help introduce a total quality control program to a company, I choose for my case study one of the company's new product development projects that is full of problems. Over the past two decades or so, this approach has proven successful.

At this level full participation in quality control and quality assurance becomes essential. Starting with those people who engage in market research and planning and ending with those employees who engage in sales and after-service, every one and every division in the company must participate.

Quality assurance with emphasis on new product development has been a success. It has ultimately led to the adoption of total quality control, which has been an effective tool in rectifying the distortions that might otherwise exist in Japanese society. There has been a need to thread the woof into Japan's vertical society, and that function has been performed by TQC.

Before I go any further, I must hasten to add that my discussion of quality control does not completely negate the importance of inspection. It must be made clear, however, that no matter how closely a company may inspect its products, there will always be some inspection misses and some defective parts will still be shipped. It is uneconomical to rely on inspection. This is the reason for shifting emphasis to process control. I do not mean to say that at the present production level the need for inspection has been obviated. In fact there has lately been a pressure to reevaluate the importance of inspection. This has come about in direct response to the issue of product liability and responsibility, which requires assembling of data for evidence.

Basically, as long as a given process produces defectives, and if inspection is possible, all items must be inspected before their shipment. Of course, the mere act of engaging in inspecting all items does not mean full implementation of quality assurance.

Similarly, no matter how well quality assurance of new product development progresses, the company must continue to exercise tight process control.

V. HOW TO DEAL WITH COMPLAINTS WHEN POOR PRODUCTS ARE SHIPPED

Poor products can be produced or shipped in a number of ways. In this section I will deal with the discovery of bad products after they have reached the hands of consumers. In other words, what kind of quality assurance measures can one take when there is a complaint or an expression of dissatisfaction from a consumer?

Another issue takes precedence over the one just discussed, however. It is the problem of a justified complaint not reaching the right person at the right time. How can this happen?

The first reason is that consumers generally do not complain. If they find fault with expensive items like cars they may complain, but for inexpensive items they do not complain. In other words, their complaints become latent or hidden, and when they buy similar products they simply switch to other brands.

We believe that if products are improved in accordance with the complaints of consumers, the consumers will continue to buy. For that reason, information concerning complaints is very important. As Diagram IV-1 shows, potential complaints must be actively changed into actual complaints. Companies must encourage consumers to complain, perhaps by using a catch phrase such as "Accepting bad products without complaint is no virtue." We created this phrase over twenty years ago, and it has since been very well received. Many people feel that manufacturers are enemies of consumers. That is not true. From the time we first began promoting QC, we have taken the stand that manufacturers and consumers must work together to make Japanese products better. Manufacturers try their best to engage in QC, but human errors do occur. We therefore ask consumers not to be docile and to say what must be said as a means of helping manufacturers create better quality products.

The second reason is that information about the complaints received from consumers and users disappears somewhere and never reaches the company or process that produced a particular product. For example, a company may maintain a sales division within its headquarters. If that division, which receives actual complaints, does not communicate complaints to the divisions of quality assurance, manufacturing, and design, that information will still disappear. Companies must develop a sure way of providing feedback on the matter of customer complaints.

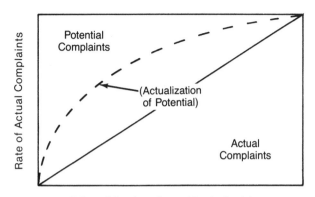

Actual and Potential Complaints

DIAGRAM IV-1

Some old-style marketing employees and managers often hide complaints trying to sweep problems under the rug. In this case actual complaints of customers become potential complaints within the company. Normally, in companies that do not have good QC programs there are ten times more potential complaints than actual complaints. These actual complaints are nothing but the tip of the iceberg.

The first step in QC is to change potential complaints into actual complaints. One must actively gather information concerning complaints and make them public. Companies which have never had QC often find that once they start QC the number of complaints increases almost overnight. This is natural. Consciously and subconsciously, people will allow things that have been hidden to surface suddenly. When a QC program is started the number of complaints inevitably increases. This increase is a clear sign of its effectiveness. If this happens in your company, take the following measures to cope with the increased complaints. You will find that as your quality improves the number of complaints will decrease very substantially.

Speed and Good Will—Exchanging with Good Products

A company must resolve to solve problems quickly with good will and let the consumer dissolve his dissatisfaction.

This means that a defective product must be exchanged with a good product immediately. Do not think that the matter is closed with this action. As I shall discuss later, you must take steps to prevent the problem's recurrence. You must make certain that defective products will never again reach the hands of consumers. For this reason, the defective product must always be retrieved to study the causes of its malfunctioning and the true state of the complaint.

In addition, you must immediately investigate products of the same variety already on the market to determine if they have the same defects. If defective products are on the market, especially if they have critical defects that threaten life or safety, all such products must be recalled and exchanged with good products. That is the responsibility of the manufacturer in performing the task of quality assurance.

Determination of Warranty Period

Make it clear that within a certain number of months or hours after a given product is sold or shipped, the company will repair it free of charge. This does not mean that the longer the period the better. People who do not know QC will say that the period of warranty or free service should be extended. However, such an extension can actually be unfair to the customers. For instance, most ladies use sewing machines only fifty or sixty hours in their entire lifetime. Thus the machines never malfunction. Other ladies sew to supplement their family income and use their machines two to three thousand hours. Naturally their machines will break down and parts will be worn. Manufacturers normally provide free repair services. This means that the price of repair is already included in the sales price. It works to the advantage of those ladies who sew to make money and against most other ladies.

I believe the consumers must be given the right to select inclusion or exclusion of repair cost in the sale price. For example, the same machine would be sold for 100,000 yen, if no free after-service is to be provided; for 120,000 yen, if three years of free service is to be provided; and for 150,000 yen, if free service is guaranteed for as long as the customer owns the machine. After-service must be considered a contract between a customer and a manufacturer. The case becomes even clearer if I point out that passenger cars and taxis cannot have the same free-maintenance agreement.

Payment of Indemnity by Contract

Any necessary provisions for indemnity must be clearly stated at the time a contract is signed.

Establishment of Service Stations

For durable goods that can be used for five to ten years, the manufacturer must assume responsibility for preventive maintenance and supplying parts in order to avoid lowering the capabilities and to provide repair in case of a breakdown. The Japanese practice is to establish a network of service stations around the world and provide well-trained service technicians in these stations. American car manufacturers leave the matter of servicing to garages and other independent establishments. Consequently they do not provide adequate service for their customers.

Owner's Manual and Checklist

Misuse, poor methods of use, or inadequate periodic checks can cause a product to become defective or to break down. Therefore for products sold, especially in the case of durable goods, directions for use and instructions for periodic checks must accompany the products. This is clearly the responsibility of the manufacturer. These documents must be written in such a way that a nonspecialist can understand and use them. Select language that a fifth-grader can understand. Write simply and clearly.

Supplying Parts for a Long Period of Time

Durable goods may be used five, ten, or even thirty or more years. As long as there are customers who use them, manufacturers are obligated to supply exchangeable parts. In the case of certain electric machines, the government decrees that exchangeable parts must be supplied for a specified length of time. Manufacturers must supply parts for a considerably longer period of time in order to gain the confidence of consumers.

VI. MEASURES TO PREVENT RECURRENCE

The most important concern in quality control and quality assurance is prevention of recurring defects. Dr. Deming spoke of a quality cycle which moves from design to production, from production to sales, from sales to market research, and then from market research to design again. It is a continuous process of designing and redesigning that raises the level of quality through prevention of recurring defects.

The general public and mass media may state that a particular mistake will not be repeated or that prevention of recurrence has been effected through QC conducted without these continuous efforts. Take these statements with a grain of salt, because they represent application of temporary measures and not permanent cures. It is easy to say prevention of recurrence, but good intentions must be accompanied by careful study followed by appropriate actions taken on the basis of that study. Without these efforts one can neither prevent recurrence, nor apply brakes to past mistakes.

The following three steps are generally considered to be measures for preventing recurrence:

    A. To remove the symptom
    B. To remove a cause
    C. To remove the fundamental cause

Actually, only B. and C. are measures for preventing recurrence, and unless one takes step C., there can be no true recurrence prevention. As for A., it is merely a temporary measure.

Let me explain using a story from my own experience. As illustrated by Diagram IV-2, a certain device was attached to a machine by means of four bolts. There was a complaint that bolt number 1 often snapped, so it was changed to a larger size of bolt. Next, bolt 2 snapped. It was decided that all four bolts should be a larger size. It looked as if the problem had been solved, but it was not. The next complaint was that an iron plate used as a holder broke into two, so a thicker iron plate was used. This company then claimed that it had succeeded in preventing recurrence of the problem.

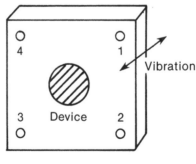

DIAGRAM IV-2

The company did succeed in removing the phenomena of the snapping bolts and the breaking plate, examples of A. above. It merely applied emergency measures. It had not done recurrence prevention.

So we studied the problem more closely. We discovered that vibration reached this device and was responsible for the phenomena of the snapping and breaking. Without removing the cause, the vibration, the company used larger bolts and a thicker iron plate. Some day the vibration would directly affect the device itself and break it. Only by removing the vibration would the company have taken a recurrence prevention measure as described in B. above. Taking a temporary measure is just like applying an ointment on a rash. The ointment may soothe the patient's discomfort, but the rash may come out again in spots all over the patient's body. This is because the cause has not been eliminated. Unless the patient's constitution changes, the rash may never disappear.

Now supposing that the vibration is removed, does it mean that C. has been fulfilled? No, it does not mean that the fundamental cause has been removed. Why was the company unable to detect vibration while testing the product during the stage of new product development? Even if the vibration were removed at the later stage, it would not prevent the problem from recurring because a similar mistake is likely to occur when another new product development takes place. Several tests were obviously made when this machine was newly developed. Why could the testers not anticipate the vibration? Clearly the tests were inadequate.

The company must reexamine its testing procedure and develop a new one which will alert to the existence of vibration that could cause snapping of bolts. The one method of preventing problem recurrence is to return to the basics and reexamine everything step by step. One must go as far back as to the development of testing procedures and their amendments during the early stages of product development. That is the only way to remove the fundamental cause listed above in C.

Speaking in more general terms, elimination of the fundamental cause is directly related to improvements in management and in important standards.

For instance, quality cannot improve if the company is only interested in considering the roles played by line workers. Quality is everyone's business, and the company must endeavor to bring about better quality in all of its divisions from design to sales and after-service. It must also seek better quality of performance from all of its workers, managers and line workers as well as sales personnel. Without taking these measures it cannot continue to make good products. This is the reason we have insisted on total quality control.

The same can be said about process control. When things went out of control in one company, its workers looked into the cause and discovered that the wrong materials had been used. They changed the materials to the correct ones and the company claimed that it had successfully prevented recurrence. This is a temporary measure, step A., and not a recurrence prevention measure. The company should have studied the reasons wrong materials had been used in the first place and should have taken appropriate actions. Instead, use of wrong materials is likely to occur again. The answer may simply be to make a check slip more legible or to change the place of storage, but these steps must be taken to ensure that no mistakes recur.

The next step is to enter into the process of lateral thinking; that is, applying similar thinking to a similar situation found in a separate environment. Are other materials stored in their proper places? Are they well controlled? By making sure that all other materials can be used properly, the company takes the first step in the removal of the fundamental cause, as stated in step C. Again, a temporary measure is not a measure for recurrence prevention. It is true that a mistake can be fixed for the time being, but that is not a cure. People who are satisfied with patchwork are the people who do not want to be bothered with the more cumbersome task of finding the true cause factors. They prefer to leave things as they are when their feeble efforts in analysis fail them.

It is said, "Once the danger passes, no more concern." Prevention of recurrence is a difficult task. The approach I have outlined is an important one in quality control and quality assurance. I believe it can be applied beyond quality control to all other social phenomena. In politics and in the personal lives of individuals, prevention of problem recurrence makes good sense. It may take time, but if applied steadily, step by step, this approach can ensure advances in our work, in our technology, and in our quality of life.

CHAPTER V

Total Quality Control

QC is the responsibility of all workers and all divisions.

TQC is a group activity and cannot be done by individuals. It calls for teamwork.

TQC will not fail if all members cooperate, from the president down to line workers and sales personnel.

In TQC, middle management will be frequently talked about and criticized. Be prepared.

QC circle activities are part of TQC.

Do not confuse objectives with the means to attain them.

TQC is not a miracle drug, its properties are more like those of Chinese herb medicine.

I. WHAT IS TOTAL QUALITY CONTROL?

Companies and individuals may give different interpretations, but broadly speaking, total quality control means management control itself.

The concept of "total quality control" was originated by Dr. Armand V. Feigenbaum, who in the 1950s variously served as company manager of quality control and company-wide manager of manufacturing operations and quality control at General Electric staff headquarters in New York City. His article on total quality control was published in the May 1957 issue of *Industrial Quality Control* and was followed by a book in 1961, entitled *Total Quality Control: Engineering and Management.*

According to Feigenbaum, total quality control (TQC) may be defined as "an effective system for integrating the quality development, quality maintenance, and quality improvement efforts of the various groups in an organization so as to enable production and service at the most economical levels which allow for full customer satisfaction." TQC requires participation of all divisions, including the divisions of marketing, design, manufacturing, inspection, and shipping. Fearing that quality which is everybody's job in a business can become nobody's job, Feigenbaum suggested that TQC be buttressed and serviced by a well organized management function whose only area of specialization is product quality and whose only area of operation is in the quality control jobs. His Western-type professionalism led him to advocate TQC conducted essentially by QC specialists.

The Japanese approach has differed from Dr. Feigenbaum's approach. Since 1949 we have insisted on having all divisions and all employees become involved in studying and promoting QC. Our movement has never been an exclusive domain of QC specialists. This has been manifested in all of our activities, including the basic QC course for engineers, Dr. Deming's seminars for top and middle management (1950), the course for foremen broadcast in 1956, and the advocation of QC circle activities in 1962. We have promoted these under various names, such as integrated quality control, total quality control, all member participation quality control, and the like. The term "total quality control" has been the most frequently used. Yet when this term is used overseas, people may think that we are imitating Dr. Feigenbaum's approach, which we are not. So I have called ours Japanese-style total quality control, but found it too cumbersome. At the 1968 QC symposium, we agreed to use the term company-wide quality control to designate the Japanese approach.

Quality Control Participated in by All Divisions

What do I mean by company-wide or total quality control? It simply means that everyone in every division in the company must study, practice, and participate in quality control. Merely to assign QC specialists in every division as suggested by Feigenbaum is not enough. In Japan the vertical line authority relationship is too strong for staff members such as QC specialists to have much voice in the operation of each separate division. To counter this situation, our approach has always been to educate everyone in every division and to let each person implement and promote QC. Our QC courses are now well defined, and separate courses are available for different divisions. For example, there are QC courses for the marketing divisions and for the purchasing divisions. After all, "QC begins with education and ends with education."

Quality Control Participated in by All Employees

Our own definition of company-wide quality control has undergone certain changes. Initially total participation extended only to the company president, directors, middle management, staff, foremen, line workers, and salesmen. But in recent years, the definition has been expanded to include subcontractors, distribution systems, and affiliated *(keiretsu)* companies. This system, developed in Japan, is quite different from what is being practiced in the West. In China Chairman Mao spoke of the inadequacy of control through specialists and advocated combining efforts of the workers, specialists, and leaders. This approach is closer to that of ours. There seems to be a common thread in the way of thinking in the Orient.

Integrated Quality Control

In effecting integrated quality control, control of quality is central, but at the same time cost control (profit control and price control), quantity control (amount of production, of sales, of stock), and control of delivery date are to be promoted. This method is based on the fundamental assumption of QC that a manufacturer must develop, produce, and sell commodities that satisfy the needs of consumers. In conducting QC, unless one knows the cost no quality planning and design can be effected. If cost control is tightly managed, one can know how much profit could be realized if certain trouble spots were eliminated. In this manner, the effects of QC can also be easily anticipated.

As to quantity, unless the exact amount is known, neither the percent defective nor the rate of reworks can be obtained and QC cannot progress. Conversely, unless QC is actively promoted—and unless standardization, the standard yield rate, standard rate of operation, and a standard workload are determined—there can be no way of finding standard cost, and consequently no cost control can be effected. Similarly, if percent defective varies too widely and if there are many rejected lots, neither production control nor control of the delivery date can be effected. In short, management must be done on an integrated basis. QC, cost (profit) control, and quantity (delivery date) control cannot be effected independently of one another. We do our integrated quality control at the core of all efforts, and that is the reason we also call this method integrated quality control. When each of the divisions (design, purchasing, manufacturing, and marketing) engages in QC activities, it must always follow this integrated approach.

In the West the definition of "quality control" has always included control of the quality of both products and services. Thus QC has been practiced in department stores, airlines, and banks. This is a sound approach. In Japan, by translating the term "quality control" into *hinshitsu kanri*, with the term *hin* connoting products, we may have unwittingly created quality control primarily for our manufacturing sector. In the past three decades Japan has emphasized quality of products, manufacturing them inexpensively and exporting them successfully, resulting in a rise in the level of Japan's living standards. In retrospect, then, it has been good to have the term *hin* (products) placed in the word designating quality.

However, I want to emphasize that the term quality means quality, and that the term extends to the quality of work in offices, in the service-related industries and in the financial sector.

I often use a diagram to explain this concept. (See Diagram V-1.) The essence of TQC is found in the central ring, which contains quality assurance narrowly defined, which means doing QC well for the company's new products. In the service industry where no manufactured goods are involved, quality assurance means assuring the quality

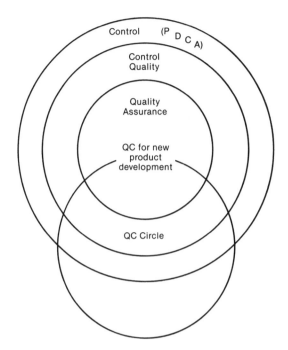

Company-wide Quality Control

DIAGRAM V-1

of services rendered. In developing new services, such as new deposit accounts or new insurance contracts, quality must be assured.

Once the meanings of QC and of good quality and good services become clear, the second ring comes into play. The ring represents control of quality that is defined more broadly, including the questions of how to bring about good sales activities, how to make salesmen better, how to make office work more efficient, and how to deal effectively with subcontractors.

If the meaning is broadened even further, the third ring will be formed. This ring stresses that control of all phases of work is to be done effectively. It utilizes the PDCA (plan, do, check, action) circle, turning its wheel over and over again to prevent recurrence of defects at all levels. This work involves the entire company, each division and each function. Each individual must also be actively involved.

Japanese QC has been fortunate in that in its history, once quality has been improved, control has been done effectively by turning the wheel of the PDCA circle. This has contributed effectively to the prevention of recurrence.

How far can a company's QC go in relation to the above three rings? That determination must be made by the chief executive officer taking into account the nature of the company. He must then communicate his decision to the entire company. Otherwise, within the company people may start debating unnecessarily about the QC definition. Some companies in Japan use the second and third rings with broader definitions. Other companies are confined to the central ring with quality assurance as the core. These can still claim to practice total quality control. One note of caution to those companies that use the broader definitions. Whatever you do, you must not forget the very essence of QC, which is found in quality assurance and in QC for development of new products.

Incidentally, QC circle activities must always be conducted as part of company-wide quality control activities. The QC circle is to be regarded as a ring that intersects all other rings. QC circle activities alone will not bring about TQC. Without participation by top and middle management and by the staff, QC circle activities cannot last. All over the world many companies are following the Japanese example in instituting QC activities. I fear many of them will not last unless they take the concept of company-wide quality control seriously and involve their top and middle management and their staff members in QC.

The above is what we call company-wide quality control or total quality control. The two terms can be used interchangeably.

II. ADVANTAGES OF TOTAL QUALITY CONTROL

Why do companies decide to institute TQC? I have given my answers in the April 1980 issue of *Engineers*, in a report entitled "Management Ideals of Companies Receiving the Deming Prize." The companies that have received the Deming Application Prize are all in the forefront of total quality control in Japan. Reproduced below is a summary of my report, outlining the reasons these companies decided to engage in TQC:

- To make our company recession proof, with true sales and technological capabilities (Ricoh Co., Ltd., recipient of the prize, 1975).
- To secure profit for the benefit of our employees, and to secure quality, quantity, and cost to obtain the confidence of our customers (Riken Forge Co., Ltd., 1975).

- To build quality into products that can always satisfy our customers. As a means of doing this, we engage in QC with (1) full employee participation, (2) emphasis on problem solving that can contribute to our profit picture, and (3) utilization of statistical approaches and methods (Tokai Chemical Industries, Ltd., 1975).
- To establish a company whose corporate health and character allow its steady growth by combining the creative energies of all of its employees, with attainment of the highest quality in the world as our goal. To develop the most up-to-date products, and to improve our quality assurance system (Pentel Co., Ltd., 1976).
- To create a cheerful workplace and show respect for humanity through QC circles with all-member participation. To supply in Japan and abroad automatic transmissions of impeccable quality, superior to the international standards but lower in cost, which takes into account fully the requirements of customers and users. To bring about prosperity of the company through improvement in management control, and thus contribute to the welfare of regional society (Aisin-Warner Limited, 1977).
- To improve the corporate health and character of our company, to upgrade quality of our products, and to raise our profit picture (Takenaka Komuten Co., Ltd., 1979).
- To establish a company whose corporate health and character are competitive and viable in any business environment change (Sekisui Chemical Co., Ltd., 1979).
- To attain the following goals: (a) Securing quality control development—To implement product goals according to company policy in a timely manner, the efforts of all employees are to be combined and organized; (b) Strengthening of control—Everyone must put into practice what he has learned about the methods and approaches of quality control and bring about improvement in the quality of control in every aspect of company activities; and (c) Nurturing human resources—To show respect for each employee as an individual, the company is to create a workplace that is worthy of everyone's labor through the nurturing and utilization of human resources and through teamwork (Kyushu Nippon Electric, 1979).

Space does not permit me to go on with other individual examples. In general, companies that have received the Deming Prize—including those not mentioned above—have the following purposes in common:

1. Improving the corporate health and character of the company—Almost all companies are serious about this point. Japan has entered a period of steady but less accelerated economic growth. So most

companies feel that they must begin again from the beginning and utilize TQC to strengthen the corporate health and character of the company. Some set specific goals. Others do not spell them out. As I have often said, QC is not an act of cheerleading. Employees cannot act if they are given nothing but abstract instructions. Top management must make clear the goals it has in mind, pointing out which part of the company's character requires modification, or which aspect must be improved.

2. Combining the efforts of all employees, achieving participation by all, and establishing a cooperative system—As discussed in Chapter 2, control by specialists does not work in Japan. All employees in all divisions must be actively involved and combine their efforts.

3. Establishing the quality assurance system and obtaining the confidence of customers and consumers—Quality assurance being what it is, the very essence of QC, most companies announce such assurance to be their goal or ideal. The difference between new-style QC and old-style management is that QC does not seek short-term profit. Its primary goal is "quality first." By doing quality assurance well, QC can gain customer confidence, which will eventually lead to long-term profit.

4. Aspiring to achieve the highest quality in the world and developing new products for that purpose—As a corollary to this, many companies speak of development of creativity, or of improvement and establishment of technology. Japan is a resource-poor country. For Japan to be able to survive in international competition, it must in a short period of time develop highly reliable products with the highest quality.

5. Establishing a management system that can secure profit in times of slow growth and can meet various challenges—After the two oil shocks, many Japanese companies attempted a number of new approaches. They included saving resources and energy, casting off debt financing of the company, and encouraging belt-tightening management. To these companies, adoption of QC brings very desirable results. Do not go through the motion of observing perfunctory QC, but consider QC to be your ally in making money. If QC is carried out effectively profit is always assured.

6. Showing respect for humanity, nurturing human resources, considering employee happiness, providing cheerful workplaces, and passing the torch to the next generation—A company is no better or no worse than the employees it has. All of the goals presented here can be accomplished through active pursuance of QC activities in the workplace, where respect for humanity must prevail. As for middle management and staff members, delegate to them as much authority as you can. Let them become "managers" in their own right. Proven

competence in QC circle activities opens the way for performing well in other management roles.

7. Utilization of QC techniques—Some people are mesmerized by the term "total quality control" and do not fully utilize the statistical methods. That is a mistake. Statistical methods form the basis of QC. Whether they be those seven simple QC tools or advanced techniques, people in the appropriate divisions must be able to master them and use them.

These seven items are the goals and accomplishments of those companies that undertook total quality control and accepted the challenge of the Deming Application Prize. I cannot be sure if they all reached 100 percent of the goals they set for themselves—the passing grade for the Deming Prize is seventy out of a possible 100—but I trust that these companies did reach 70 percent of their goals.

III. WHAT IS MANAGEMENT?

Goals of Management

My view of management is as follows. (See Table V-1 on the following page.)

1. People

In management, the first concern of the company is the happiness of people who are connected with it. If the people do not feel happy and cannot be made happy, that company does not deserve to exist.

The first order of business is to let the employees have adequate income. Their humanity must be respected, and they must be given an opportunity to enjoy their work and lead a happy life. The term "employees" as used here includes those employees of subcontractors and affiliated sales and service organizations.

Consumers come next. They must feel satisfied and pleased when they buy and use goods and services. If a television just bought breaks immediately, or if an electric heater is the cause of fire and injury, then the company that sold it has done enormous disservice. Also, if at the time of purchase the salesman does not treat the customer with courtesy or fails to explain fully how the merchandise is supposed to work, the customer will not be satisfied.

The welfare of shareholders must also be taken into consideration. Japan is a capitalist society, and each company must make sufficient profit to provide stock dividends for shareholders.

TABLE V-1

OBJECTIVES AND TECHNIQUES OF MANAGEMENT			
Goals	People		
Techniques	Quality	Price Cost & Profit	Quantity Date of Delivery
Physics			
Chemistry			
Electrical Engineering			
Mechanical Engineering			
Civil Engineering			
Architecture			
Metallurgy			
Mathematics			
Statistical Methods			
Computer			
Automatic Control			
Production Engineering			
Industrial Engineering			
Time Study			
Motion Study			
Market Survey			
Operation Research			
Value Engineering/Value Analysis			
Standardization			
Inspection			
Education			
Material Control			
Equipment Control			
Measurement Control			
Metallurgical Tool Control			
.....			

Companies exist in a society for the purpose of satisfying people in that society. This is the reason for their existence and should be their primary goal. We must now deal with the question of how to reach this goal.

There are three basic means which enable us to reach this primary goal. They are quality, price (including cost and profit), and quantity (including the date of delivery). I shall call these three our secondary goals. Controlling these three must be considered the goal of a given company, a process I shall call goal control.

2. Quality

I have discussed quality repeatedly. Defective products will not only inconvenience consumers but also hinder sales. If a company makes too many products that cannot be sold, it will waste raw materials and energy. This waste will also be a loss for society. A company must always supply products with the qualities the consumers demand. Consumers' requirements usually get higher and higher year after year as society advances. What was good last year may not be adequate the following year. In QC narrowly defined, QC means controlling carefully the supplying of quality products that have good sales points.

3. Price, Cost, and Profit

Everything has to do with money. No matter how inexpensive a product, if its quality is poor, no one will buy it. Similarly, no matter how high the quality, if the price is too steep, again no one will buy it. The consumer's main demand is for a just quality at a just price.

It is said that in a capitalist society, making profits is the goal of a company. On the other hand, there are some people who say that profit is sinful. These two statements represent extreme positions and both of them are wrong. If there is no profit, there can be no development of new products and new technology. Nor can there be investment in equipment modernization. Without profit, no salaries can be paid, and good people will not come to work for the company. In the end the company will be bankrupt, inconveniencing the very society it is supposed to serve.

Profit is actually the means to maintain a company permanently. A company without profits cannot even pay its fair share of taxes, and cannot fulfill its social obligations.

To raise profits, cost control must be practiced effectively. First, there must be a cost plan. At each stage of the development of a new product, the wheel of the PDCA circle must be turned in the right direction.

Generally, if QC is conducted effectively, defectives will decrease, and waste of materials and time will also decrease. This will lead to a rise in productivity and as a result will bring cost down. Through this process, products can be supplied to consumers at just prices. Incidentally, the price of a product is not determined by the cost but rather by value of true quality.

4. Quantity and Date of Delivery

A company must manufacture products in the amount required by the consumers and it must supply them to the consumers prior to the specified delivery date.

Quantity control includes control of the following: amount purchased, amount of production, amount of materials and products in stock (including amount of products in the production process), amount of sales, and date of delivery. If the company is overstocked with a certain commodity, a lot of resources and capital are not being utilized. Not only are they wasted, but they also push up the production cost. Of course if the amount of stock is too low, the company will not be able to meet adequately the requirements of consumers. The famed *kanban* (just-in-time delivery) system at Toyota takes this factor into account. It is a system that has been completed after effective implementation of QC and various forms of quantity control have taken place. Without these safeguards and effective control, a premature introduction of the *kanban* system can spell disaster, causing a complete shutdown of a factory.

On the other hand, if people, quality, cost, and quantity are effectively controlled, management can proceed smoothly.

Techniques and Tools of Reaching Management Goals

There are many techniques and tools that can be used to reach management goals. The items listed vertically in Table V-1 are these techniques or tools.

For example, physics, chemistry, mathematics, and mechanical engineering are all tools. At the annual convocation of my Institute, I often say to my students, "You are going to study many subjects, such as physics, chemistry, mathematics, electrical engineering, and mechanical engineering. You are engineering students, but to study these subjects must not in itself be the purpose of your entering this institute. You are to study these subjects as a means of serving society, the nation, and the world. In your learning, never make the mistake of confusing the true goal with the means."

Misperceptions are found not only among students but also among their professors. They study statistical methods and computers, but the study becomes the end in itself. In the case of quality control, when it was first introduced in Japan, there was a similar tendency. Some people thought quality control existed for the sake of statistical methods, while others thought that it existed for standardization. They confused the goals with the tools. Japan's quality control has become what it is today only after it has learned to correct past mistakes.

The tools of quality control are often divided into two categories, proper techniques and control techniques. I do not particularly like this differentiation. In Table V-1, items such as mechanical engineering, electrical engineering, architecture, civil engineering, metallurgy, physics, and mathematics are proper techniques, and statistical methods and the items listed below are considered control techniques. In my view, they are proper techniques as well.

To attain the four goals described earlier, we must utilize all proper techniques at our disposal and produce high quality goods inexpensively to serve our society.

I ask all applied scientists and engineers to acquire technology which is more like A. than B. in Diagram V-2. I call B. the well-type technology and A. the cone-shaped technology. When products become complex and technology becomes highly specialized as in today's world, the well-type technology becomes structurally frail. It dries up too quickly and cannot contribute to true technical development or to the development of new products. One must acquire cone-shaped technology, which develops a greater width as one digs in deeper. For example, a mechanical engineer must possess a general knowledge of electrical engineering, electronics, metallurgy, chemistry, statistical

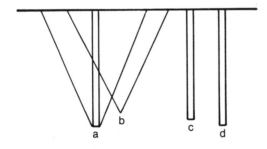

A. Cone-shaped   B. Well-type

DIAGRAM V-2

methods, and computers. If an engineer has only well-type knowledge he cannot move from project c to project d. However, if he has cone-shaped knowledge, once he succeeds in new product development in a, he can transfer that knowledge to new product development in b.

Let us try another example. What makes good engine specialists? Obviously engine specialists must be good mechanical engineers, but they must also know metallurgy and casting to appreciate how raw materials for the engine are made. They must be familiar with the principle of engine operations and must be able to utilize some degree of technical knowledge in the following areas: machine processing technique, fuel and lubricants, packing, ignition, electronics, statistical methods, computers, standardization, etc.

Similarly, to create the highest quality products, we must utilize all tools and proper techniques available to us.

I am often asked, "What is the relationship between quality control, industrial engineering, and operation research?" My answer is simple: "To create a quality product, we utilize all tools at our disposal, including industrial engineering and operation research." The so-called QC techniques (statistical methods) are, of course, the tools. However, QC itself must be treated as one of the basic objectives of the company. "Do not confuse objectives with the tools."

CHAPTER VI

TQC
Is a Thought Revolution
in Management

If TQC is implemented company-wide, it can contribute to the improvement of a company's corporate health and character.

QC is one of the major objectives of the company. It is its new management philosophy.

Set your eyes on long-term profits and put quality first.

Destroy sectionalism.

TQC is management with facts.

TQC is management based on respect for humanity.

QC is a discipline that combines knowledge with action.

I. THOUGHT REVOLUTION

As discussed in Chapter 1, one of the reasons I began QC was:

"The eight years that I spent in the nonacademic world after my graduation taught me that Japanese industry and society behaved very irrationally. I began to feel that by studying quality control, and by applying QC properly, the irrational behavior of industry and society could be corrected. In other words, I felt that the appplication of QC could accomplish revitalization of industry and effect a thought revolution in management."

To associate revitalization of industry with a thought revolution in management may sound somewhat excessive. But that expression represented the goal to which I aspired. Many companies had transformed themselves after applying QC. The manner in which they were transformed may be classified in the following six categories:

1. Quality first—not short-term profit first
2. Consumer orientation—not producer orientation. Think from the standpoint of the other party
3. The next process is your customer—breaking down the barrier of sectionalism
4. Using facts and data to make presentations—utilization of statistical methods
5. Respect for humanity as a management philosophy—full participatory management
6. Cross-function management

II. QUALITY FIRST

If a company follows the principle of "quality first," its profits will increase in the long-run. If a company pursues the goal of attaining a short-term profit, it will lose competitiveness in the international market, and will lose profit in the long-run.

Management that stresses "quality first" can gain customer confidence step by step, and the company's sales will increase gradually. In the long-run, profits will be substantial, and will permit the company to have stable management. If a company follows the principle of "profit first," it may obtain a quick profit, but it cannot sustain competitiveness for a long period of time.

These things are easier said than done. In practice, many companies are still operating on the basis of profit first. They may proclaim "quality first," but at the shop they are only interested in cutting cost. Some people still fear that raising quality means raising cost, which in turn will reduce profit. It is true that cost will rise temporarily when the quality of design is upgraded. However, the immediate trade-off can be found in the company's ability to satisfy the requirements of consumers and to meet competition in the world market.

The additional advantages are not difficult to find. If the "quality of conformance" improves, defects become fewer and fewer, and the "go-straight-percentage" increases. There will be a substantial decline in the amount of scrap, in reworks, in adjustment, and in the inspection cost. This will bring about a very substantial cost saving, accompanied by higher productivity. Without this benefit, automation of the process becomes virtually impossible, and factories operated by robots become inconceivable. In fact, improvement in the quality of design is the first step toward higher sales and profits and lower cost.

This truth is made abundantly clear in Japan's competition with the United States in the markets for automobiles, color televisions, integrated circuits, and steel. Only recently have some Americans begun to realize this fact. In many areas, America is still governed by an old-fashioned capitalism. The owner, the chairman, or the directors are the ones who scout and hire a new president. The president thus chosen must show a quick profit or else may be fired. He has no time to think about long-term profit. He is forced to choose a short-term profit, and in so doing loses his match with the Japanese.

In the case of automobiles, American manufacturers did produce compact cars before 1970 to compete against the Japanese. However, the profit from a large-sized car came to from five to ten times that of a compact, so American manufacturers worked on their compact cars only half-heartedly. When the need arose, American consumers bought Japanese-made compacts irrespective of price because of their reliability and fuel efficiency.

In steel, in automobiles, and in integrated circuits, American companies have not been able to make the investments in equipment that they need in order to seek long-term profit. They have lagged behind in plant modernization. In addition, the Securities and Exchange Commission requires that reports be issued every three months. This relatively recent development has further contributed to the myopic views of American managers.

Some managers in the United States are simply tired of managing, so they sell their companies to enjoy their retirement. What is lacking is their concern for their social responsibility and the welfare of their employees. Society suffers from their unconcern and the companies are also affected because they cannot be expected to attain long-term profit.

Generally speaking, the higher the manager is on the corporate ladder, the longer must be the period used for evaluating his work. In the case of the president, marketing division head, and manager of the factory, evaluation must be based on their work extending over a period of three to five years. Without this safeguard, these people may seek only short-term profit, and neglect both quality and equipment investment. It is a sure way to lose long-term profit for the company.

III. CONSUMER AND NOT PRODUCER ORIENTATION

We have always taken the position that companies must manufacture products that the consumers want and are happy to buy. The aim of QC is to implement this basic approach. We have continuously stressed this since the inception of QC in 1949, so there is nothing new in this statement. In practice, however, unscrupulous people seem to find ways to counter this thought revolution. Pride and obstinacy may also be factors, but in any event, some companies plainly choose the path of producer orientation contrary to the consumer orientation that we suggest. This trend is especially noticeable in a seller's market, in a closed market that does not permit trade liberalization, and in a monopoly market. In such markets, producers make and sell products that they consider to be good without paying any attention to the requirement of consumers.

Example 1: It tastes good to me but not to the consumers.

    A. The senior managing director is over 60 years old. He makes candy according to his own taste. The candy's primary market group is teenagers between the ages of 15 to 20. How can an old man of 60 know the taste of young men and women?

    B. The shop had worked hard to produce margarine but its sales had remained poor. Market research, utilizing specially designed experiments and sensory testing, revealed that consumers did not like the taste.

In both of these instances, producers have considered their own taste paramount, disregarding the likes and dislikes of the consumers.

Example 2: We never expected that our customers would use our products that way.

This is an utterly irresponsible statement by those designers who do not try to know how consumers use their products.

Example 3: One company received a large number of complaints about its electric wire without knowing how consumers were using it. How can a manufacturer provide quality assurance under such circumstances?

An electric wire factory manufactured electric wire according to company specifications. However, complaints kept coming in about the wire sold. An investigation uncovered unsatisfactory performance in the factory's wire winding equipment, speed, after-treatment temperature, and insulation oil. The factory then made changes in company specifications.

A logical reaction to the consumer orientation approach is always to think in terms of another party's position. This means to listen to their opinions and to act in a way that will take their views into account. This principle also applies in international trade. For example, American car manufacturers have to lay off a large number of their workers due to sluggish sales. Most of the responsibility rests with management; it is really not the responsibility of Japan. However, if the United States is indeed suffering from the loss of trade, Japan must take America's position into consideration and extend helping hands to solve the problem, provided such an act does not violate the anti-trust law.

IV. THE NEXT PROCESS IS YOUR CUSTOMER

The phrase "the next process is your customer" could be incorporated into the previous passage where we discussed consumer orientation. However, in a company where sectionalism is strong, this approach can be so important that I have decided to treat it separately.

I invented the phrase "the next process is your customer" while working with a steel mill from August 1950 to September of that year. Example 1 explains the situation.

Example 1: We were trying to work out a solution to the problem of reducing the number of defects and scratches in steel plate, and the following exchange took place:

ISHIKAWA: Why not call in the workers in the process next to yours and the one before yours to investigate?

DIVISION CHIEF: Professor, do you mean to say we should call in our enemies?

ISHIKAWA: Wait a minute. The next process should be your customer. Why do you call them enemies? Every evening go to the plate mill that is your next process and ask, "Are those ingots we delivered today satisfactory?" That should create better relations.

DIVISION CHIEF: Professor, we can never do that. If we go to the next process unannounced, they will think we are spying on them. They will immediately chase us out.

Example 2: What is the proper role of the staff? Who is the customer of the staff?

Generally speaking, there are two tasks that the staff must perform. The first is to work as general staff. Staff members make plans and submit proposals to the president and the factory manager. The second task is that of the service staff. Staff members must consider the first line divisions, such as the design, purchasing, manufacturing, and marketing divisions, as the next process and serve them. I believe that a typical staff member should work thirty percent of the time as general staff, and seventy percent as service staff.

The trouble with most staff members is that they consider their work to be devoted one hundred percent to the general staff work, so they act as if they were members of the military General Staff. They act on the erroneous assumption that they should operate the entire company. They have no notion of serving line workers and divisions but rather give orders and constantly fight with the first line of company activities, divisions that should be the staff's customers. Conversely, line workers and divisions never listen to the staff. In war days, we used to speak of the acrimonious relations existing between the General Staff Headquarters and the Kwantung Army posted in Manchuria. The situation I have just described resembles it.

Within a company, the divisions of general affairs, personnel, accounting, production engineering, and quality control devote seventy percent of their time to serving their "customers," the line workers and divisions. Similarly, the staff must always consider what kind of service it can perform for the line divisions. The accounting division may erroneously feel that it is the only one engaged in profit and cost control, but the line divisions are actually the ones that are engaged in profit and cost control. The role of the accounting division is to provide data to these divisions to make their work of profit and cost control easier. That is the service they can perform effectively. My advice to people in line divisions and QC circle leaders is this: "Make the company staff work for you as much as possible."

Example 3: Corning Glass Headquarters' organization (1958-1980).

I visited Corning Glass in 1958. Its organization chart for the headquarters had the term "service" printed everywhere. For example, there was a Service Accounting Department, a Service Engineering Department, a Service Quality Control Department, etc. The vice-president in charge of all of these departments had the title Service Vice-President. I asked why the term "service" was inserted as a prefix. The response was that unless the term "service" was placed there, people would forget that they were there to serve and would become rather arrogant.

Company-wide quality control cannot be complete without total acceptance of this kind of approach by all workers. Sectionalism has to be broken down, and the company has to be ventilated so that everyone can enjoy a breath of fresh air. Everyone must be able to talk to each other freely and frankly. That is the spirit of TQC.

One final thought on this issue. The customers, that is, workers in the next process, can make a request of the preceding process only if the request is reasonable and based on facts and data.

V. PRESENTATION WITH FACTS AND DATA: USE OF STATISTICAL METHODS

Facts are important and their importance must be clearly recognized. After this is done, try to express these facts with accurate data. The final step is to utilize statistical methods to analyze the data, which will enable you to make an estimate, pass judgment, and then take appropriate action.

QC is often called fact control, but people frequently ignore this. People do not look at the facts carefully, and the data they submit are not reliable. At times, they ignore the facts and rely on their own experience, sixth-sense, and gut feelings.

1. Facts

The first order of business is to look at the facts. A common fault among engineers is to have a preconceived notion in their minds and play with data to match it while ignoring the facts. To such engineers, my suggestion is to join the work process (e.g., assembly line) and quietly observe it for one week to ten days. Without knowing what is going on in the work process, engineers cannot adequately perform their duties.

2. Turning Facts into Data

The next step is to translate facts into data. But the danger here is that the right data may be difficult to obtain. This is the reason I say, "If someone shows you data, consider them suspect. If someone shows you measuring instruments, consider them suspect, and if someone shows you chemical analysis, consider it suspect."

In brief, there are three ways of looking at this issue. They are

- False data
- Mistaken data
- Inability to obtain data

A. *False data*

Unfortunately, there are many false data being used in industries and in society. I observed this problem in one factory. The factory manager said to me, "The trouble with our company is that whenever I tell my superiors the truth they become angry with me." That same factory manager lost his temper when a young engineer working for him told him the truth!

False data are generated through this process.

Why is false data created? Often superiors are at fault.

1. The superior does not know how to think in statistical terms and does not have a sense for dispersion. So whenever the data vary a little, he thinks that something has gone wrong and becomes angry. Those who work under him are scolded although they do their job adequately. To protect themselves, they have to lie and write false reports.
2. When mistakes are made, anywhere from two-thirds to four-fifths of the blame lies with the superior or the superior's staff. Only one-third or one-fifth of the responsibility rests with those who work under him. But usually, the subordinates are the ones who will be scolded. So they submit false data.

Unless the superior changes his way of thinking when situations similar to those in 1. and 2. arise, one can never expect total elimination of false data.

When workers make mistakes and funny data appear, the superior must not immediately report that to the upper level management or scold his subordinates. Instead, he must work with his subordinates to prevent recurrence of the problem. If this is done, incidence of false data will diminish.

B. Mistaken data

Almost as soon as I began the work of quality control, I became aware that data were collected erroneously because the people engaged in it did not know proper methods. For example, they were not familiar with the sampling method and measuring method and collected data that were either wrong or useless. So I asked the Union of Japanese Scientists and Engineers to establish the Sampling Research Committee for them. This effort has been bearing fruit, but there are still some knotty problems in actual application.

Similarly, because definitions for defects, defectives, reworks, and adjustments are not clearly stated, mistaken data emerge in the number of defective products, percent defective, rework rate, adjustment rate, and the "go-straight-percentage."

C. Inability to obtain data, inability to measure

It is true that we have advanced technology, but there are many problems that defy measurement. With regard to quality, true quality characteristics cannot be measured for a large number of products. For example, the ease in driving and the comfort and style of a passenger car are quality characteristics that cannot really be measured.

We must study these problems to establish methods of measurement. But when that is impractical, we must inspect products by using the sensory testing method and then accumulate the results into statistical data.

3. Utilization of Data and Statistical Methods

Many books on SQC and QC devote a great number of pages to this subject, so here I shall try to be brief.

First, we must realize that by performing process analysis and quality analysis without fanfare for a long period of time, we have been able to bring about progress in Japanese technology. Many people say that proper techniques have brought about progress in technology and control techniques have sustained it, but this is wrong. It does not make much sense to divide technique into proper techniques and control techniques. Western nations are better than the Japanese in this regard, for they are not very much concerned with this distinction.

My feeling is that the so-called control techniques are also proper techniques. By using whatever techniques are available to us we have been able to bring about improvement in quality, cost reduction, and efficiency. Process analysis and quality analysis have been done effectively through the application of QC. We have been able to export not just manufactured goods and hardware but also our technology and software.

The second point I wish to emphasize is this. If a manager does not utilize data and statistical methods, and relies only on his own experience, sixth sense, and gut feelings, he is admitting that his company does not possess high technology.

Improvement in the management's attitudes is an important by-product of utilization of facts, data, and statistical methods.

VI. RESPECT FOR HUMANITY AS MANAGEMENT PHILOSOPHY

When the management decides on company-wide quality control, it must standardize all processes and procedures and then boldly delegate authority to subordinates. The fundamental principle of successful management is to allow subordinates to make full use of their ability.

Industry belongs to society. Its basic goal is to engage in management with people in the center. Everyone who is connected with the company (consumers, employees and their families, shareholders, subcontractors, and employees in the affiliated distribution system) must be able to feel comfortable and happy with the company, and be able to make use of his capabilities and realize his potential. Profit first is an old-fashioned idea that must be discarded.

The term humanity implies autonomy and spontaneity. People are different from animals or machines. They have their own wills, and do things voluntarily without being told to by others. They use their heads and are always thinking. Management based on humanity is a system of management that lets the unlimited potential of human beings blossom.

One of the basic ideas that motivates QC circle activities in the workplace is to create a "workplace where humanity is respected."

Top managers and middle managers must be bold enough to delegate as much authority as possible. That is the way to establish respect for humanity as your management philosophy. It is a management system in which all employees participate, from the top down and from the bottom up, and humanity is fully respected.

The Swedish people have observed the way we handle management. They termed it "industrial democracy." That says it all.

VII. CROSS-FUNCTION MANAGEMENT, CROSS-FUNCTION COMMITTEES

In 1960 I prepared a dual chart illustrating cross-function management by divisions and by functions. (See Table VI-1 and Diagram VI-1.) This was adopted by the Toyota Motor Company. It has been modified and has been used at Toyota with continued success. The full story is contained in an article written by Mr. Aoki of Toyota (*Statistical Quality Control,* February–April, 1981).

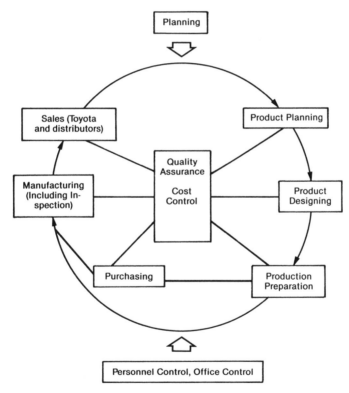

Concepts of Cross-function Management—I

DIAGRAM VI-1

Japanese society is often described as a vertical society, and its industries share this structure. Industry has a strong top-to-bottom vertical bond while sectionalism hinders development of horizontal relations. For example, no matter how hard the division of quality assurance attempts to perform the function assigned to it, it cannot do so adequately within the existing organizational structure.

Cross-function management which has cross-function committees for support can provide the woof to help the company run crosswise, making possible the responsible development of quality assurance.

In textiles, the warp by itself remains a thread. Only when the woof is added, and when warp and woof are intertwined, will there be cloth. In a company, the analogy holds true. A vertical society resembling the warp is not an organization. It becomes a strong organization only when various functions such as quality assurance are intertwined with the warp as the table illustrates. Organizational management is possible only through the intertwining of the warp, which engages in management by divisions, and the woof, which engages in control by cross-function management.

When we speak of cross-function management, many topics immediately come to mind, including quality assurance, quantity control, cost (profit) control, new product development, control of subcontracting, sales control, and the list can go on and on. From the perspective of company goals, the main functions are the three functions of quality assurance, cost (profit) control, and quantity control. To these three may be added personnel control. All others are auxiliary functions defined by the steps to be taken or the means to be adopted.

In accordance with the functions to be managed, the company must establish cross-function committees. For example, a cross-function committee on quality assurance may be established. The chairman must be a senior managing director or a managing director who is in charge of that function. Committee members are selected from among those who hold the rank of director or above (if necessary, division heads may be included). The number should be around five. It is not desirable to select committee members only from among those who are directly connected with that specific function. Actually, it is better to have one to two persons from nonrelated divisions as committee members. Each cross-function committee must maintain a secretariat within the division that handles the function under consideration, and appoint a secretary. The committee must be operated flexibly. When dealing with major functions, the committee must establish regularly

TABLE VI-1

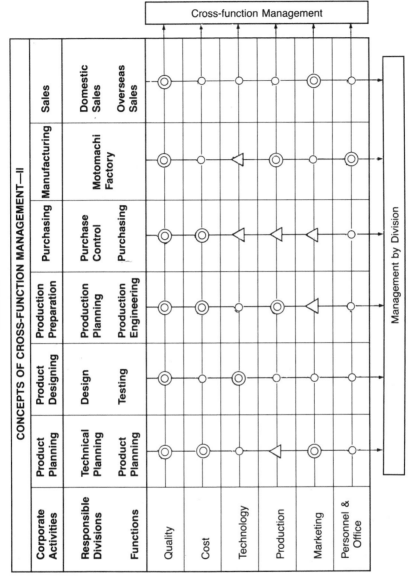

CONCEPTS OF CROSS-FUNCTION MANAGEMENT—II

scheduled monthly meetings which can engage in the audit of functions under study. The committee may also establish project teams under it.

The committee then allocates responsibilities and authority for quality assurance to all affected divisions in concrete terms. It creates a viable system of quality assurance and establishes applicable rules.

Every month the committee must study the conditions of quality assurance and determine if any claim has been registered against defective products. It must revise and redetermine the allocation of responsibilities periodically. At Toyota the monthly meeting of the cross-function committee does all of these things efficiently. (Please keep in mind that the company has had about ten years of experience in cross-function committees before reaching this stage.) The committee's meetings are formal ones. In contrast, the management conference above the committee makes reports but does not make policy decisions.

The committee, however, does not implement quality assurance. Nor does it assume direct, day-to-day responsibility for quality assurance. That task is performed by each of the line divisions in this "vertical society." The responsibility of the committee is to let the woof be woven into the warp to strengthen the entire organization. Examples of effective and ineffective uses of cross-function committees are given below.

Misunderstandings and Problems Connected with Cross-function Committees

1. Some companies convene a meeting only when there are problems. They consider cross-function committees to be project teams and ad hoc in nature. That approach must be avoided. Committees must be established as standing committees and have regular meetings. They study the system and provide the woof. Without them there can be no sound horizontal structure for the company.

2. Some people erroneously assume that once cross-function management is established, the company can dispense with control by division. Both are necessary.

3. Some people feel that all specialists and all affected divisions must be included in the committee. No, the cross-function committee is of a higher order than that.

4. Do not regard cross-function committees as your project teams. Let us assume that you have a cross-function committee for profit control and your profits have not reached an established goal. Does your

committee establish quotas for the line divisions to reach certain profit goals? No, these are to be determined by the line divisions themselves (through their management by objectives).

5. Initially, company directors who are named committee members tend to represent only their sectional interests in their capacities as heads of the design division, accounting division, etc. This must not be allowed to happen. What they must strive for is to build a company-wide perspective from the outset.

6. Some people may genuinely believe in their devotion to the functions to which they are assigned, but continue to interpret everything that comes before the committee in terms of their own divisions. For example, a cross-function committee on quantity control must be concerned with the overall product amount for the entire company. However, a committee member from the production control division may not pay any attention to events in other divisions. Similarly, an accountant on a cross-function committee on cost control may forget the overall picture and only discuss accounting procedures.

7. The work of cross-function committees cannot go smoothly unless information is gathered routinely through all channels within the company.

8. Do not increase the number of cross-function committees excessively. When there are too many committees, they may engage in inter-committee disputes and create a situation very similar to inter-divisional rivalries.

Another thing that has to be kept in mind is that there must be a thought revolution in the company in favor of cross-function management, otherwise the committees created for that purpose will remain committees in name only. In a company where the tendency for authority to move from the top down, where the president exercises absolute power, the need for cross-function management is far more important than in other companies. Yet it is precisely in this kind of situation where it is most needed that it has not been operating very smoothly.

Effectiveness of Cross-function Committees and Cross-function Management

1. Company officers no longer think in terms of their narrow sectional interests but become true managers with broader perspectives. They become company directors worthy of the name. Their way of thinking becomes more flexible, and they tend to help one another more.

2. Quality assurance and quantity control are cross-functionally more effectively conducted on a company-wide basis.

3. Inspections are conducted across the divisions, so there is very little need to increase the number of divisions and sections.

4. Line workers also become conscious of cross-function management, which results in better communication between processes and divisions. Human relations among the workers are also enhanced.

5. It becomes much easier for those in the subordinate positions to submit proposals and suggestions.

VIII. COMPANY-WIDE QUALITY CONTROL AND IMPROVEMENT IN TECHNOLOGY

False notions about QC still abound in our society, in our industries, and among individuals. People claim that QC will stifle creativity and hinder improvement in technology. They also maintain that QC seeks only preservation of the status quo. These misunderstandings are caused by the word "control," which gives the impression that changes are not to be welcomed. Unfortunately, these people cannot perceive QC as a tool for bringing about a thought revolution.

Japanese intellectuals and journalists are beginning to appreciate the importance of QC, but only after it has been fully reported in mass media overseas. This is unfortunate, but I shall not complain. I prefer to let the results of our work speak for themselves. We must avoid the cacophony that usually accompanies journalism.

As QC activities have become widespread, group psychologists want to get a part of the action. There are theorists who create Theory X, Theory Y, and Theory Z and provide their critiques of our activities. My response to them has remained the same. "All of such theories are contained in our QC circle activities. We do not present them as theories, however, we simply practice them."

QC can be a theory, but at the same time it is a practical discipline. I urge people who are connected with QC not to become mere theorists or mere practitioners. They must become experts as both.

When I first became involved in QC, my aim was to help improve Japanese technology through QC and TQC. That was the thought behind the cause and effect diagram. In order to do process control, I became a strong supporter of process analysis, which then led me to on-line computer control. It was more than two decades ago that I engaged in quality analysis for newsprint rolls. We apply the same methods today, and through process analysis and quality analysis, causes and effects are becoming clearer. In other words, by engaging in QC effectively, one can establish a solid foundation for technology. Lately Japan has been experiencing an upsurge in its technology exports, although still remaining a net importer of technology. Perhaps through QC this situation can also be rectified.

I wish to close this chapter by repeating an old goal which I set for myself in engaging in QC, TQC and CWQC.

"As I perceive it, the goals of new quality control are to be as follows: First we must export good and inexpensive products in large quantities to make the Japanese economy stronger and to solidify the foundation of its industrial technology. Second, through quality control, we must enable Japan to export its industrial technology in order to solidify Japan's future economic base. And finally, as far as companies are concerned, they must reach the position where they can rationally divide their profits three ways, among consumers, employees, and shareholders, and as far as the nation is concerned, we must improve the living standards of our people."

CHAPTER VII

Dos and Don'ts for Top and Middle Management

If there is no leadership from the top, stop promoting TQC.

QC cannot progress if policy is not clear.

Organization means clarified responsibility and authority. Authority can be delegated but responsibility cannot.

QC cannot progress without attacking middle management.

Strive to become a person who does not have to be always physically present at the company, but become a person who is indispensable to the company.

A person who cannot manage his subordinates is not half as good as he is supposed to be. When he is able to manage his superiors, then he can be called an accomplished person.

I. AN APPEAL TO TOP MANAGERS

Unfortunately, there are many top executives, especially chief executive officers, who do not have a taste for total quality control. Many of them probably will claim that they understand QC, but QC is an acquired taste. Taste is acquired only after eating. A chief executive officer can appreciate the taste of QC only after he has taken active leadership in its implementation. In this chapter, I am going to describe what is expected of the top management, especially of the chief executive officer.

In speaking of top management, I wish to emphasize that the term should not be interpreted too broadly. If only one or two company directors are dedicated to total quality control, that is quite insufficient. Unless the person in charge, the one who has the full power, that is, the president or the chairman, takes the initiative and assumes leadership in implementing quality control, the program cannot succeed. In Japan if you say something to a director, he will say, "please communicate that to the managing director." If you say something to a managing director, he will say, "please communicate that to the senior managing director or to the president." A director does not direct, but is often directed, and seldom is he really in the position to speak for the top management.

II. MISUNDERSTANDING COMMON TO TOP MANAGEMENT

Top managers often have little or no understanding of total quality control. Here are some examples.

We graduated from quality control.

As long as a company manufactures and sells products, quality control must be implemented for the duration of that company's existence. For the company to grow and advance continuously, it must engage in the task of improving corporate health and character continuously. This can be accomplished through QC. This fact must always be kept in mind by the executive considering QC.

Not much interest in quality.

Top managers are always interested in profit, sales, investment in plant and equipment, financial manipulations, and political dealings, but they exhibit very little interest in quality, which is at the core of everything. In distribution systems and other service industries people tend to think that quality is merely a concern of those who are engaged in manufacturing. What I am saying here is borne out by the fact that there are not many companies that have long-range plans for quality or for QC, and that most of them do not know the level of their product or service quality in relation to that of other companies or of other countries. We find that in management quality, quantity, cost (profit), and human factors are all important. But top managers who are not concerned with quality do not realize that lately the relative weight of quality has become very great. They often make the mistake of thinking that improving quality means to raise the cost. This comes from the faulty notion that QC equals inspection.

We don't need QC.

Some people will say, "We are making plenty now. Why do we need QC?" or "Our sales are up, up, up. Who needs QC anyway?" They obviously do not know how total quality control in Japanese companies is being handled, and they simply do not know what QC is all about. Or they may be conducting their own old-style QC, relying on their own experience. These people overlook the fact that, for the sake of the company, QC must be organizationally sound and lasting.

My suggestion to these executives is that they talk with presidents of companies that have been very successful through implementation of total quality control.

We have specialists handling QC. I am sure we are doing just fine.

This statement proves one thing—top managers are unfamiliar with QC and are not assuming the necessary leadership. They do not know the truth about their own quality or about QC.

We emphasize education. Our people are sent to seminars in and out of the company.

These people erroneously assume that by giving education to employees, everything is taken care of in total quality control. It is true that education is important, as it is said, "QC begins with education and ends with education." But education alone does not make QC work. People may attend seminars and become educated in QC, but executives are not aware that these people are often not given opportunities to utilize the knowledge thus acquired.

We started QC a little over ten years ago and are doing fine.

These executives think that the length of time is all that counts. This can lead to mannerism in QC. They either do not know the truth about their own company or about QC, or are simply saying something they do not truly believe. Quality changes and advances constantly. Quality that was good a year ago may become poor the following year. Don't rest on the laurels of a Deming Application Prize received five or ten years ago. There is a continuous stream of new employees replacing old employees who retire. The same company does not have the same employees that it had a few years ago. A company such as this must pay close attention to what is going on now, this very minute. To do so, a QC audit by the top management, that is the president, is suggested.

Commanding cost cutting, forgetting quality.

Top executives love to order cost cutting, considering it the ultimate purpose of management. Of course it is important to cut cost, and QC can eventually lead to a substantial cost cut. But if the executives seek only a short-term cost advantage, which QC cannot provide, and allow lowering of quality and reliability to occur, it will result in the loss of long-term customer trust in the company. Executives often speak of quality first, or the priority of quality, but in reality they are only interested in cost.

My products have the best quality in Japan.

This is a statement typical of short-sighted top executives whose perspectives do not extend beyond Japan. They somehow forget that trade and capital liberalizations are now a reality. Japan must import natural resources, of which she is poorly endowed, and must export more to pay for the imports. Top executives must always observe what is taking place in the world and be concerned with quality levels all over the world. This is the spirit of a slogan that was adopted for quality month in 1966. "Open your eyes to the world, but solidify your home market with QC."

Lack of understanding has also produced the following attitudes: "QC means making inspections more strict." "QC means implementing standardization." "QC is statistics." "To practice QC is to study something very difficult." "Let the inspection section or QC section handle QC." "As long as the factory does well in QC, nothing more is needed." And "QC has nothing to do with the headquarters, administrative division, or sales division."

III. WHAT MUST THE TOP MANAGEMENT DO?

Study quality control and total quality control ahead of anyone else in your company, investigate how they are implemented in Japan, and have a good understanding of the issues involved.

Studying alone will not bring out the taste for quality control. Practice QC for two or three years, and you will then know the taste and appreciate it. The more you chew, the tastier the food, and so is QC.

Establish policies defining the positions the company will take in regard to total quality control.

Top management must determine the positions the company will take in regard to total quality control. (For a discussion of the forms the company can take, consult Chapter 5.) It must establish policies in regard to TQC's introduction and promotion and the general attitudes surrounding it. Policies thus established must be disseminated throughout the entire organization and implemented by all workers, from top management down to line workers. In any event, these policies must deal with the rationalization of management, the re-vitalizing of the company, and the desire to manufacture products with the highest quality in the world.

Assemble information concerning quality and QC and specify, in concrete terms, the priority policies in regard to quality. Establish "priority of quality" and "quality first" as the basic policy, and determine long-term goals for quality standards. This must be done in concrete terms and with an international perspective.

To establish a long-range plan for developing new products is one of the fundamental functions of management. In performing this task adequately, targeted quality standards and design quality standards become an important concern. But too few executives are interested in this subject, and if they ignore quality they cannot expect their employees to show interest in quality.

Assume leadership in quality and QC. Always be a vanguard promoting them.

Just issuing policies does not do anything for the company. Top management must be in the forefront of activities and assume the leadership position. Check what has been accomplished, and provide guiding hands. From the time the top executives of a large company show an understanding for total quality control, issue policies, and assume leadership to the time these policies penetrate through to line workers, anywhere from three to five years will elapse. By that time there will have been an improvement in corporate health and character, and the company will have reached the Deming Application Prize level. In the case of small companies, if TQC activities are well-organized, the time needed may be merely one or two years. Thus TQC decisions must not be carried out as if the movement will be of short duration. TQC must be implemented for as long as the industry is in existence. One must therefore have a long-range view and patience accompanied by a sense of continuity. It is often useful to write and apply for the following as a means of promoting QC: Evaluation for the JIS Mark, the Director of Regional Bureau of MITI Award, the Minister of International Trade and Industry Award, and the Deming Application Prize. However, a note of caution is in order. QC must not be implemented for the purpose of receiving awards and prizes. QC conducted in that manner is likely to attach too much importance to form. It will only harm the company without achieving visible advantages.

To implement QC, provide adequate education and combine it with long-range plans such as personnel placement and organization plans.

Quality control is a thought revolution in management, and it must be conducted as such. It is said that "QC begins with education and ends with education." Education through formal seminars must be carried out 150 to 200 percent. In other words, one and one-half to two seminars must be scheduled for each person. It is common to assume that one seminar will suffice, but people will forget and old habits will return. Investment in education pays off and can be returned 100 to 1,000 times as results pour in from many different quarters.

Education through formal seminars can be only one-third or one-fourth of total education. The remainder must be carried out through day-to-day work in which the superior educates his subordinates. Delegating authority is also a form of education. In the past, companies did not emphasize the responsibility of a superior to educate his subordinates. There were superiors who would delight in the mistakes of their subordinates while refusing to enlighten them with their own hard-earned experiences. That was unfortunate, and must not be allowed to happen again.

Some companies do not consider combining their personnel placement and organization plans with their education plans. These plans are actually very closely related. The results of lack of coordination are illustrated in the following example: A company spent a large sum of money to send one of its employees to a QC Basic Course with a view to making him a staff member for QC in one of the company's sections. But as soon as he finished the course, he was reassigned to another section. The division that needed him for its QC could not proceed as originally planned.

Check to see if quality and QC are conducted as planned, and take action.

To do so, organize a system that will routinely provide necessary information concerning quality and management which can be fed back to the top management. One of the characteristics of Japanese TQC is that it engages in quality audits and diagnoses the state of QC control. I strongly urge the institution of QC audits by the top. The CEO or the person with the highest authority may be responsible, otherwise it is essentially meaningless. (See Chapter 11 for further details on this subject.)

Make clear the responsibility of top management over quality assurance. Equip your company with a solid system of quality assurance.

Quality assurance is the very essence of QC. At any stage of total quality control, if quality assurance for products is not handled well TQC will not be any better than a castle built on sand. Therefore the responsibility of top management over quality assurance must be made clear. When a new product is developed, assign responsibility for quality assurance throughout the company for each step of the way. Make certain that there is a quality assurance system, and that information on it is fed back to the top smoothly and quickly. To ensure this I suggest establishment of a cross-function committee for developing new products and another one for quality assurance to engage in cross-function management. Also make sure that issues of *Quality Monthly* and *QC Monthly* reach the top.

Establish your own system of cross-function management.

Japanese industry has a strong vertical top to bottom command structure. However, its horizontal communication leaves something to be desired, being hampered by the existence of strong sectionalism. One of the points emphasized in total quality control is horizontal communication between divisions. Japanese industry is very much like the traditional *noren* (a curtain hung in the doorway with the name of the shop on it; it is usually slit twice to give an appearance of three separate curtains). It hangs well vertically but does not have common threads horizontally. The lack of the woof, or rather the lack of integrated management, has been one of the weaknesses of Japanese industry. Organization means to thread the woof, and it can be carried out by the application of cross-function management. Cross-function management must be promoted in the areas of personnel, quality assurance, profit (cost), and quantity (date of delivery). I have already dealt with cross-function management in the preceding chapter.

Drive home the notion that the next process is your customer, providing assurance for each successive process.

One of the greatest principles behind QC is consumer satisfaction. Within a company, the next process is the customer. If this way of thinking is driven home, the walls of sectionalism will crumble and fresh air will breeze through the company.

In Japanese industries where sectionalism is strong, top management must constantly teach all employees that the next process is the customer. Each preceding process must learn to serve the process following it. It must assure product quality as well as work quality. Once this has been accomplished, comments like the following will be heard: "Since implementing QC, the company has become well 'ventilated'." "Everyone can now speak frankly." "We now have a common language." A word of caution to the staff: Don't forget that "line workers are your customers."

Top management must assume leadership in bringing about a breakthrough.

Within a company, it is easy to become satisfied with the status quo. This holds true for workshops and offices (design, research, purchasing, production, and marketing divisions), which can be "feudalistic" in their orientation. But ours is the age of rapid technological innovation and worldwide competition. If the top management cannot assume leadership in breaking through the existing barriers, their company is going to be left behind. Japanese people used to think of caution as a virtue and said, "A cautious man taps a stone bridge before crossing." The question for our age is how fast one can cross the bridge after tapping. The age of excessive caution is over. One who cannot enter the new age by crossing the bridge cannot be a top manager.

Top managers must establish clear-cut goals and guidelines that deal with the issues of which consumer groups (including those overseas) the company wishes to serve, and what capabilities the company wishes to assign to the product, at what production cost, at what volume of sale, and at how much profit.

IV. ROLES OF MIDDLE MANAGEMENT

The positions occupied by the middle management, that is, division heads and section chiefs, are important ones. They are also difficult jobs both for the individuals concerned and in terms of vertical and horizontal relations.

In Japanese management, the terms "division heads and section chiefs" are used rather indiscriminately. There are many different kinds of people and positions designated by this term. The difference is significant between a company that is in a growth industry and continues to expand, and a company that has seen its best days and is not expanding. The difference is also noticeable between large corporations and middle- and small-sized companies. The people can vary widely, in terms of personality, in terms of age, and in terms of years of service. There can be a section chief in his twenties as well as a section chief in his fifties who is near retirement. (Note: some companies retire their employees as early as age 55 as part of their "lifetime employment" package.) A more recent trend is to give the title of section chief to people who perform specialized functions, without assigning them subordinates.

In some companies, rotation is uncommon, and the same division head or section chief may have been in the same workplace for a long period of time, knowing everything there is to know about the place and being more like a skilled worker than a chief. Other division heads and section chiefs are following an elite course set for them, and their present positions are merely a step toward the company directorship. Hereafter, we shall use the term "middle management" or "middle managers" to represent these division heads and section chiefs.

Some middle managers are given considerable authority, perceive of their roles to be managerial, and act accordingly. Some will work their heads off when commanded, but do not make plans or submit recommendations to the top. Some have confidence in their own judgment while others have none. Some transmit commands from above straight through to those who are below, serving as a channel. Some transmit commands in such a way as to serve their own purposes. Some never transmit any command that is injurious to their own narrow interests. From those who can transmit commands effectively, to those who do not, there is no uniformity at all in performance.

The same can be said about these managers' reactions to QC. There are some middle managers who are enthusiastic about QC

There are others who dislike it without having experienced it. There are those who can never say if they are for QC or against it. There are some who can be effective as specialists but who cannot manage subordinates. The quality of middle management differs, influenced by each company's history and system as well as by individual personalities. It is impossible to treat all middle management under one heading, but I shall make generalizations nevertheless, forgetting the differences and treating managers as human beings who have many things in common.

Traffic Policeman

The example may not be exactly appropriate, but in a sense the routine that a middle manager must perform within the company is like that of a traffic policeman. He stands at crossroads that run horizontally and vertically. He must channel information to those who are above and those who are below, and to those who are in related divisions or sections. At times he may have to give a stop signal or tell a car to turn left or right. If a car violates the rules, he must issue a warning. His job is to see that traffic moves smoothly and that the work of the company is conducted safely. He must look around his four corners and use his own judgment to assess conditions.

If a traffic policeman is not careful, he can create a traffic jam by blowing his whistle incessantly. It may even result in a traffic accident. People will say that the traffic tie-up was caused by the policeman, and that it would be better just to have traffic signals.

A traffic policeman cannot see beyond the four corners, or he may simply refuse to see things beyond his immediate surroundings. If he has information about the next intersection or about traffic conditions a mile or two away, he will be able to control the traffic better. He must therefore go beyond his immediate surroundings to obtain crucial information and acquire the ability to make judgments based on a broader perspective.

Let us consider the example for a moment. Is it always necessary for a traffic policeman to stand at an intersection? If the volume of traffic is low, traffic lights will suffice for most intersections. Only at rush hour or in an emergency will the policeman (or middle manager) be needed. If a policeman appears unnecessarily when traffic lights are doing an adequate job, he wastes his efforts and hinders the traffic flow (work) in spite of the hard hours he puts in. And when he is really needed, he is so tired that he no longer can do his work!

Strive to become a person who does not have to be always physically present at the company, but become a person who is indispensable to the company.

This is the message I convey to my students before their graduation. It may seem self-contradictory, but it is not. The first part suggests
that subordinates be trained well to know the policies and feelings of
the manager. If they also learn to work together harmoniously, then
the manager need not be physically present in the company. This
message encourages the creation of workplaces where trust in subordinates is the rule.

The latter part means simply this. When something very important happens in the company, for example, a challenging new product
or market is created, or a number of difficulties comes up, make
yourself indispensable for such occasions. Become a person with
wisdom and fighting spirit, so that when the time comes, others will
plead, "Please return to the company. We need you."

*One who cannot manage his subordinates is not half as good as he is supposed to
be. When he is able to manage his superiors, then he can be called an
accomplished person.*

This is my favorite saying. The first half is self-explanatory.
However, do not use your position to check and scold your subordinates and cause them to work for you reluctantly. That is not good
management. Instead, build up your subordinates' trust in you and let
them know what you are thinking. Make them happy and willing to
work for you.

The phrase "managing one's superiors" may be objectionable to
some. What I mean is that you should work in such a way that your
superior will accept your opinions and recommendations. In this way
they will continue to work for you.

There are many different types of superiors. With some, even if
what you say is right, your opinion may not be accepted immediately.
To persuade someone in the position of authority, you must have the
right data, right knowledge, and right opinion. But having all of these
is not in itself sufficient. People are human and have their own
positions and feelings. Then there is the factor of mutual trust; for
example, does the person who is presenting a recommendation have
the trust of his superior? Does the latter have a positive feeling toward
the former? The person making the recommendation must also have
the power of persuasion. Generally a middle manager can be considered well-established in that position if his recommendations are
accepted one after another by his superior.

Of course, one cannot force an opinion on a cautious superior. That could hardly be called managing. When dealing with superiors who are strong-willed, I suggest that you repeat your recommendations three times. This does not mean that you voice that opinion once today, once tomorrow, and once the day after tomorrow. That will end in a fight. If your recommendation is not accepted the first time, use the following checklist to reconsider your presentation:

- Was there anything wrong with my thought process?
- Did I possess adequate data?
- Did my presentation have flaws in it?
- Did I pick the right moment to speak to him?
- Did I present it with conviction?
- Did I take into account his position?

You can make your second presentation after a cooling-off period, and only after you have adopted a new method of persuasion based on new information. If after three times the superior still does not accept your recommendation, then you must drop the matter. After all he is your superior. In my experience, however, even a dictatorial and inflexible president will listen to an opinion presented three times. When I spoke about this to a director of a certain company, he commented, "Well, in my case, I ignore any opinion which is presented to me just once." This approach of course has its own flaws.

Middle managers are sandwiched between the top and bottom and must act accordingly to fulfill their responsibilities.

At the first QC Circle Conference held in 1963 one of the leaders was a woman who had obtained remarkable results through the cooperation of her section chief. When questioned, she answered, "That's why I am so busy. One-half of my job consists of prompting my boss with data, using them like a whip on the rump of a horse." Well said indeed.

If you delegate authority freely your subordinates will use their abilities to the fullest extent and grow in their jobs.

The boss has the responsibility of educating his subordinates. He must impart his knowledge and experience to his subordinates through on-the-job training (OJT).

Some middle managers take the position that it is very difficult to teach something that took them ten or twenty years to learn. Instead of teaching their subordinates, they delight in seeing the subordinates make mistakes. Good work can never come out of this. Unless subordinates are well-trained and reliable, a division cannot be adequately managed. And only with adequate management can the person in charge look forward to greater things.

A word of caution—Education must not be confined to verbal instruction and good training. The ultimate goal is to see that subordinates become self-sufficient in their jobs. In teaching, do not hammer at the same point over and over again. That can be annoying to the subordinates. Choose your approach carefully.

Another educational method, and a very important one, is to delegate authority and let the subordinates handle the matter as they see fit. In rapidly expanding companies, one notices that young middle managers work diligently, effectively, and with enthusiasm. The fact that these companies do not have enough middle management personnel may have contributed to this rather vigorous and youthful delegation of power. In contrast, in companies that are not expanding, many middle managers are merely wasted. In my case, almost immediately after my graduation I was named a technical officer in the navy and worked in a naval ordnance factory for two years. One year after graduation I was given command of 600 people to build a factory on a 245-acre site. That was a great learning experience.

Show your subordinates your basic policy, and if needed give some words of advice, but otherwise simply delegate authority and let them handle the job. If they make mistakes, that is a small price to pay for the growth you can expect in them. After all, every failure is a stepping stone to success. In a company managed dictatorially, trouble usually begins after the strong chief executive retires. Trouble occurs because the executive has neglected to educate his subordinates and there has been no delegation of authority. Failure comes to the company where people are not nurtured.

Don't always look to the top when working.

In some companies employees always look to the top when working. This phenomenon is found frequently in companies where there are exceptionally strong executives whose management style is dictatorial. In one company I know of, all employees, including senior managing directors, looked to the top in doing their work. What does this mean? In an extreme case, a company can become a place where no one does any work unless there is a command or order from the president. If the president gives a command, everyone works hard to carry it out; if he doesn't, no one works. The company has neither a battalion commander nor a troop commander. In other words, from senior managing directors down, everyone in that company is a private.

In the Russo-Japanese War of 1904–05, the Japanese army relentlessly attacked the Russian position in Port Arthur called 203 Hill. I call this type of company a 203 Hill-type company. Under the command of the president, everyone makes a dash at the enemy and occupies the hill, but casualties are very heavy. What that company needs is to have battalion commanders, troop commanders, and platoon commanders who use their heads. When I see a company with a 203 Hill tendency, I advise company executives: "Create an atmosphere in which your senior managing directors will be able to express their opinions freely to the president, directors to senior directors, division heads to directors, section chiefs to division heads, and so on. If you can accomplish this, your company will be able to engage in total quality control and improve its corporate health and character." But this is unfortunately easier said than done.

Middle managers and those below are responsible for getting the right handle on the facts concerning the workplace.
    Unless one can obtain facts and accurate data about the workplace, there can be no control or improvement. But gathering facts is a very difficult task. There are many lies and many false data. Why is this so? People supply false information:

- To put the best foot forward
- To hide mistakes
- To make sure not to be disadvantaged
- Unknowingly and unconsciously

But I wish to emphasize that sixty or seventy percent of the responsibility for producing lies and false data resides with superiors. Why are their subordinates prone to telling lies? Here is a list of reasons:

a. Unreasonable orders
b. Quick-to-anger superiors
c. Annoying interferences
d. Dictatorial control by headquarters and superiors
e. Lies by the superiors
f. Superiors who cannot accept statistical dispersion and have no understanding of it
g. Lack of good regulations and operation standards
h. Poor systems of personnel evaluation
i. Superiors who always shift blame

j. Superiors who give orders, orders, and nothing more

k. Poor methods of checking, or inadequate checking

These and other reasons create false data in Japanese society and industry. Accompanying them are mistaken data and false data consciously or unconsciously created. It is the task of the middle management and managers below them to purify these data, ensuring their accuracy and enabling the company to know the true facts.

The late Mr. Nabeshima, president of Sumitomo Electric Industry made this observation: "One of the most important reasons for having the president conduct QC audits and receive reports of QC activities is to enable the president and others to know the facts. Any of us in the company with the rank of section chief or above must work on the basis of data given to us. If the data are wrong, management is not possible." This observation demonstrates how difficult it is for top management to obtain accurate information.

When I was in the business world, working in a company, my section chief always checked the daily report. One of his objectives was to correct the data. A young technician noted the true data concerning the yield on a graph. The section chief scolded him, "Don't you know the yield for this process is seventy percent? Don't give us that extra number." Another time, one factory manager told me, "Confidentially, Professor Ishikawa, what I have here is the true monthly report. We send the other report over there to the headquarters." I have also encountered many times unreliable sales figures provided by different sales offices.

Just who is responsibile for these situations? It seems to me that top management must bear the greater part of the blame.

Who hinders a company's breakthrough?

For a company to grow, it needs to break through the barrier of status quo. Once a person becomes a division head or a section chief, however, he may feel that he has it made. He may feel that there is no point in taking risks that will endanger his position. This attitude is unavoidable among some division heads and section chiefs. But if there are too many middle management people like these, the company does not have a bright future. Please note, however, that one-half of the responsibility rests with the top management, who have made their middle managers into non-risk-takers.

It is the responsibility of middle management to make QC circle activities work.

We shall be dealing with this topic in the next chapter. But here I simply want to state that QC circle activities are the mirror capturing the reflection of middle management. Middle management can either make QC circle activities take fire, or leave the torch unlit.

Communicating with other divisions—cross-function management.

As discussed earlier, the strong vertical command structure in Japanese society and industry has inhibited growth of horizontal communication, and sectionalism has been prevalent. Interdivisional communication and cross-function management are not synonyms, but they can be considered together for the purpose of discussion. If we investigate the function of quality assurance horizontally, what comes to light is the inability of many divisions to coordinate their activities. This observation applies to many divisions, from planning, design, testing, evaluation, production engineering, purchasing, production, and sales, to the after-service division.

One of the tasks of middle managers is to find a way to bind these divisions horizontally, and to coordinate their activities along functional lines. To achieve interdivisional cooperation one cannot fight with the previous process or the next process or with another division. The middle management must also strive to foster better personal relations among themselves.

The key to success is to look into the future. The president must look ten years into the future, the director five years, the division head three years, and the section chief must look at least one year into the future.

A manager must manage his own division well and solidify his immediate surroundings. That in itself is an important task for him. But in his thinking, he must always look to the future. He must be forward-looking and engage in vanguard control. I have suggested that a division head look at least three years into the future, and a section chief one year. This will train them to develop a broad perspective about their industry while performing their duties for the company. However, some middle managers, and in some instances even top management, worry continually about what took place yesterday or last month. Their outlook is backward-looking. That can have an unhealthy effect on their subordinates, who may also become backward-looking. A company that must always move onward and forward cannot afford to be wound in such a skein.

Space does not permit me any further elaboration. But briefly, I wish to urge middle managers who occupy important positions in their companies to be proud, self reliant, and courageous. Use the suggestions supplied above and study diligently to achieve self-development and mutual development.

CHAPTER VIII

QC Circle Activities

Only when foremen and line workers assume responsibility for process, can QC become successful.

People in the front line are the ones who have the facts down pat.

QC circle activities provide mirror images of the abilities of the president and middle management.

QC circle activities that are consistent with human nature can succeed anywhere in the world.

Where there are no QC circle activities, there can be no TQC activities.

I. QC EDUCATION FOR FOREMEN

Since 1949, when we first established a basic course in quality control, we have endeavored to promote QC education across the country. It began with the education of engineers, and then spread to top and middle managers and then to other groups. However, it became clear that we could not make good quality products by merely giving good education to top managers and engineers. We needed the full cooperation of the line workers actually making the products. This was the beginning of the journal *Gemba-to-QC* (or *QC for Foreman*, referred to as FQC, first issued in April 1962). With the publication of this journal, we began QC circle activities.

When the FQC journal was first published, I became chairman of its editorial board and issued the following policy statement:

1. Make the contents easy for everyone to understand. Our task is to educate, train, and promote QC among supervisors and workers in the forefront of our work force. We want to help them enhance their ability to manage and to improve.

2. Set the price low to ensure that the journal will be within the reach of everyone. We want as many foremen and line workers as possible to read it and benefit from it.

3. At shops and other workplaces, groups are to be organized with foremen as their leaders and include other workers as their members. These groups are to be named QC circles. QC circles are to use this journal as the text in their study and must endeavor to solve problems they have at their place of work. QC circles are to become the core of quality control activities in their respective shops and workplaces.

I also insisted on voluntarism. My view was that QC circles are not to be conducted at the command of a superior but must be conducted voluntarily in individual workplaces. If workers do not wish to participate, that is fine. Do not force them. On the other hand, I encouraged properly constituted QC circles to be registered with the journal and have their names published. Employees feel a sense of satisfaction and responsibility when they see their names in FQC. As of December 1983 there were 173,953 QC circles and 1,490,629 QC circle members registered with the QC Circle Headquarters. I do not know how many circles are not registered. My guess is that there are ten times as many circles currently in operation that are not registered.

To promote QC circle activities on a nationwide basis, and to do it efficiently and accurately, the QC Circle Headquarters was established in 1963. Nine QC Circle Regional Chapters were organized in 1964 and thereafter. These organizations published journals and books, made slides, and conducted seminars, lectures, and correspondence courses. These activities were organized for the purpose of promoting self-development among the practitioners of QC. We also created the term "mutual development" for which, aside from QC circle activities, we organized the QC Annual Conference for Foremen, the QC Circle Conference, mutual visits and discussion among QC circles, the QC Circle Cruising Seminar, and the dispatch of the QC Circle Overseas Study Team (FQC Team). Japan has been able to boast great success in QC activities. This has been possible because of our relentless pursuit of excellence in these organizations.

II. BASICS OF QC CIRCLE ACTIVITIES

As QC circle activities gain momentum and their number increases, many activities that bear no resemblance to QC circles may start using the same name. Thus it becomes necessary to give a clear-cut definition of what a QC circle is and what its aims are. To answer these questions, the QC Circle Headquarters published *The General Principle of the QC Circle (Koryo)* in 1970 and *How to Operate QC Circle Activities* in 1971. The basics of QC circle activities, helpful to individual QC circles, are contained in these two volumes. The following are excerpts from these two books, in the English version prepared by the QC Circle Headquarters.

1. What is the QC Circle?
   The QC Circle is
       a small group
       to perform quality control activities
       voluntarily
       within the same workshop.
   This small group carries on
       continuously
       as a part of company-wide quality control activities

> self-development and mutual development
> control and improvement within the workshop
> utilizing quality control techniques
> with all the members participating.

2. Basic Ideas behind QC Circle Activities

The basic ideas behind QC circle activities carried out as part of company-wide quality control activities are as follows.

1. Contribute to the improvement and development of the enterprise.
2. Respect humanity and build a worthwhile-to-live-in, happy, and bright workshop.
3. Exercise human capabilities fully, and eventually draw out infinite possibilities.

The above list shows fundamental ideas behind QC circle activities. In addition, I cite ten items as useful guides in conducting QC circle activities: (1) self-development, (2) voluntarism, (3) group activity, (4) participation by all employees, (5) utilization of QC techniques, (6) activities closely connected with the workplace, (7) vitality and continuity in QC activities, (8) mutual development, (9) originality and creativity, and (10) awareness of quality, of problems, and of improvement.

The basic ideas behind the QC circle are contained in these ten items. I shall now proceed to explain some of them.

Voluntarism

Some of our young people, the postwar generation, are becoming too dependent on others. They do their work reluctantly because they are told to do so. The underlying assumption is that unless they are told to, they will not work, and this spinelessness and lack of independence are unfortunately increasingly pronounced. Specialists in behavioral sciences may come up with different and often complex definitions concerning human nature, but as an engineer I provide a simple answer. Machines and animals are different from people. The first difference is found in the fact that people have their own wills and they can do things voluntarily. If they do things because they are told to do so, then they are no different from machines and animals. The second difference is in the fact that people use their heads. They think and they have the brains for storing knowledge and creating ideas.

When we first started our QC circle activities, we decided to make the circle into an activity that would respect voluntarism. Our movement was to be one based on respect for humanity. That was not possible without our insistence on voluntarism. Thus, as described earlier, we do not force our activities on others. Join if you wish, but our basic principle has always been that there can be no coercion from above. Of course, a company is an organization, and it cannot permit everyone to do his own thing. When we speak of voluntarism, we accept the constraint that each member is a member of a given society and company and must abide by the rules and policies set forth in the particular organization. I emphasize this because so many companies forget that voluntarism is the key to success. They may command that everyone join QC activities. Under certain circumstances commands may be necessary, but once the activities are at the takeoff stage, this policy of command must be quickly changed. Unless employees can feel that they are participating in the activities of their own free will, they cannot succeed.

In an ideal form of democratic management, the systems operating from the bottom up and from the top down are well coordinated. If only one of these systems is emphasized, it never works.

Self-Development

Literally, self-development means studying on one's own. Our emphasis has always been on raising people's abilities through education and training as a means of promoting total quality control. The education level in Japan is high, and people's abilities will rise steadily if education, training, and self-study are all allowed to continue. However, there are many people who stop learning once they leave school. I often say to my students graduating from college, "A period of true learning begins right now." But some will respond, "Do we have to study after we graduate?" This is a very unfortunate attitude.

I insist on both education and training. If we are to emphasize only one, then problems can arise. Training is often understood in the West to mean technical training. Technical training alone is not adequate for our purpose.

Mutual Development

We have been emphasizing mutual development since we first began QC circle activities. Workers tend to be nurtured in their own sectional environments and have narrow perspectives. We wanted to give them broader perspectives, making them see things from the standpoint of the corporation as a whole or even have a worldwide perspective. We wanted them to think and to exchange ideas with those in other workplaces, in other companies, and in other industries. We established QC Circle Conferences, fostered mutual development and discussion in QC circles (organized between different companies and industries, allowing participants to visit the workplaces of other industries and companies and to raise questions and discuss topics of mutual interest), sent QC circle teams overseas, and conducted overseas seminars. All of these activities were for the purpose of mutual development.

Some workers may not respond to the suggestion of their superiors that they engage in QC activities. Once they are exposed to QC meetings and exchange ideas with others, however, they may come to realize, "We are behind; we had better do something about it." Division managers and section chiefs can dispense with preaching to their workers. They would do well to send potential QC leaders and members to those places where mutual development is encouraged. Let employees find out on their own. One of the reasons Japan's QC activities have grown this far is that we have so many opportunities for mutual development. Human beings are willing to do things when they discover the need on their own. They are reluctant when they are told to do so by someone else.

Participation by All the Members

"Participation by all the members" means that if there are six persons in one workplace, all six of them must participate in QC circle activities. It does not mean that all employees in a given company must participate in QC circles.

However, here is a word of caution. Total quality control, of course, means that all employees and all divisions participate. However, it does not mean that everyone in the company from the president down must belong to a specific QC circle. There are some who will create special QC circles and through them participate in the company's total quality control program. On the other hand, some managers and technicians may participate in the program through the normal functions assigned to them.

To return to the case of the six persons in one particular workplace, participation by all six is imperative. If even one person decides not to participate, the QC activities cannot function smoothly. This is often the most difficult problem faced by the leaders in programs that are just beginning.

There are three stages of participation by all the members. The first stage is to have everyone join a specific QC circle. The second stage is to have everyone attend QC circle meetings. For this purpose, leaders must find a time and place suitable for everyone. The final stage is to engage in activities with each member assigned a particular task. When all three stages are completed the QC circle becomes fully participatory.

Continuity

QC circles are not to be maintained for a given period and then abandoned. As long as there is a workplace or a company, the circles must be continued. Many companies appoint teams to improve certain aspects of company operations and dissolve these teams once the problems are solved. We call these teams by various names, such as project teams, QC teams, or task forces. We must clearly differentiate these team activities from QC circle activities.

It has been more than twenty years since we first began promoting QC activities in Japan in 1962. From the beginning we wanted the activities to be a continuing project, and this hope has been realized. To insure continuity, one must not act in haste but be patient. In the long life of QC circle activities, there will be inevitable ups and downs and discouraging slumps. There will be times when members simply feel like quitting. Be patient, and overcome such temptations by creating QC activities that are conducted on even higher levels.

We established the QC Circle Grand Prize in 1971. It is awarded each year in November at the meeting of the All-Japan QC Circle Conference. Fourteen QC circles recommended by the regional chapters receive gold medals or silver medals. The most important criterion in the selection of these circles is their continuity. According to the regulations established by the Conference Committee, the circle eligible to receive the prize must have been in continuous operation for at least three years, and each circle must have solved at least two themes per member of the circle. Thus, if a given circle has six members, it must solve a total of twelve or more themes before becoming eligible for the prize. After observing the circles that have received the prize, I can say that they are the ones whose members continually seek to solve problems. In the process, all are also enriched by valuable cooperative experience.

III. HOW TO START QC CIRCLE ACTIVITIES

In this section I will provide some pointers on how to start QC circle activities. Before that can be done, however, it is necessary to clarify QC circles' relations to the company-wide quality control program.

One of the premises in starting QC circle activities is that total quality control is being implemented in the company. In the past, companies have usually started total quality control first and then begun QC circle activities. Lately, however, small- and medium-sized enterprises and companies in service industries, such as banks, distribution organizations, and hotels, tend to begin with QC circle activities and then attempt to introduce total quality control afterwards.

Conditions are not similar from company to company or from one type of industry to another. One can of course begin with QC circle activities, but one must keep in mind that QC circle activities are merely part of an overall total quality control program and cannot have separate existence from it. Thus even if one starts with QC circle activities, if there is no prospect for combining them with total quality control they cannot last. Even if they do for a brief time show success, it cannot be a true success. For instance, employees at the lower ends of the hierarchy may work hard to make their QC circle activities succeed while top and middle management and their staff neglect total quality control. There would be no encouragement for those engaged in QC circle activities to continue.

Now as to the steps to be taken in initiating QC circle activities, I consider the following to be appropriate:

1. Managers, division heads and section chiefs, and those who will be responsible for QC must be the first ones to start studying about QC and QC circle activities.

2. They must attend QC circle conferences and visit industries and companies that are implementing QC circle activities. Make provisions for foremen and future circle leaders to have these same opportunities.

3. Select a person who is going to be responsible for promoting QC circle activities in the company. This person is to study about QC and prepare a simplified text for the training of QC circle leaders and members.

4. The company then begins recruiting circle leaders and gives them training in QC and QC circle activities. Do not teach them things that are too difficult. The curriculum may be confined to fundamentals of QC circle activities, how to look at quality, how to look at quality assurance, how to look at control and how to improve it (PDCA or

plan, do, check, action), and how to look at statistical methods. As to the seven tools of QC, the cause and effect diagram, Pareto chart, histogram, check sheet, and stratification principle will suffice. Anything beyond these can be taught when QC circle activities are well on their way.

5. The leaders, thus trained, return to their workplaces and organize QC circles. The number of people in a given circle must be limited to ten or fewer. The best group is often made of three to six people. When the number is too large, participatory elements of the circle activities suffer.

6. Initially, foremen can be the most suitable QC circle leaders. As the activities progress, however, it is best to make the leadership position an elected one, irrespective of position in the company. When a circle is started with a large number of participants, divide them into smaller groups, such as subgroups and mini-groups. As for their leadership, make sure that there is an adequate system of rotation.

7. Leaders will then teach the members what they have learned. They must take time to do this and utilize the data and problems existing in their immediate workplace to explain. If necessary, the person promoting QC in the company may assist in this educational process, but the best approach remains one of the leader teaching his own group. To teach is to learn, and from the very experience of teaching his members the leader will also learn a great deal.

8. After studying and after gaining a basic understanding of QC, the members then select a common problem that is close to them in their own workplace as the theme of their investigation. This is the beginning of QC circle activities. The theme is to be selected by the leaders and members in close consultation with one another but without interference from other quarters. At first they may not find it easy to know what they are doing. There are times when superiors or the promoter of QC in the company may be consulted about the theme to be investigated. But voluntarism and independence must be the guides. One caution: the superior must be notified of the theme thus selected. Workers must be able to identify problems existing in their own workplace without being told by others. This is the reason for my stress on voluntarism and independence. Incidentally, once QC circle activities are well on their way, it becomes easier and easier to identify problems.

IV. HOW TO IMPLEMENT QC CIRCLE ACTIVITIES

To implement QC circle activities in Japan, the following three points must be taken into consideration: (1) how to promote QC circle on a nationwide scale, (2) how to promote it in a company, and (3) what can an individual QC circle do?

How to Promote QC Circle on a Nationwide Scale

Japan has a QC Circle Headquarters as well as regional chapters. While there is a nationwide network of QC circle organizations, they are not connected with the government or with its various bureaus. All of these QC circle organizations are private and voluntary. There are a number of countries whose governments sponsor introduction of QC circle activities. For example, in South Korea and China QC circle awards are provided by the government. QC circle activities differ from country to country. Suffice it to say that the voluntary aspects of Japan's QC circle activities have served the nation's interest well.

In Europe and America QC has taken form as activities handled by consultants. They do not have specific QC circle headquarters that can engage in study, in further investigation, and in planning future activities.

To set the record straight I must add that Japan's QC Circle Headquarters is the headquarters for QC circle activities and is not the headquarters for total quality control activities. At this point there is no national headquarters for TQC. TQC is promoted by interested parties in cooperation with the Union of Japanese Scientists and Engineers and the Japanese Standards Association.

How to Promote QC Circle in a Company or Office

The first order of business is to establish or select a division that is to be responsible for promoting QC circle activities. Then select a person who will be in charge of that division. If the company already has a division of quality control, QC circle activities can be placed under its jurisdiction. Avoid the division of labor seen in some companies where total quality control is handled by the quality control division and QC circle activities are handled by the personnel division. That is contrary to our aims.

The division thus selected oversees all QC circle-related activities, including a company-wide QC education plan, QC circle conferences, intra-circle conferences, and a system of making awards and accepting suggestions. If people are to be sent outside the company to observe QC activities, this division makes the selections and necessary arrangements. The success or failure of QC circle activities often depends on the determination of the top management, on their selection of the person in charge of QC promotion, and on their collective enthusiasm. Select the individual wisely!

What Can an Individual QC Circle Do?

There are a number of problems each of the circles must face. Each must select its own theme independently and then engage in the task of solving problems attached to this theme. At that time, the following "QC story" becomes very useful:

1. Deciding on a theme (establishing goals)
2. Clarifying the reasons this particular theme is chosen
3. Assessing the present situation
4. Analysis (probing into the causes)
5. Establishing corrective measures and implementing them
6. Evaluating the results
7. Standardization, prevention of slipups, and prevention of recurrence
8. After-thought and reflection, consideration of remaining problems
9. Planning for the future

These nine steps, which we call the "QC story," were initially designed to make the reporting of QC activities easier. But the steps contain far more than that. If an individual circle follows these steps closely, problems can be solved; the nine steps are now used for the problem-solving process.

Quality control circles engage in their activities along the lines suggested by these steps, and when they reach their goals they make public their experiences at QC circle conferences. Their talks, of course, follow the outline set by these nine steps.

Heretofore, company reports have contained only the results of their procedures, reflecting on the attitude that it is the results that really count. These are operational reports. In QC reports, we place emphasis on 2, 3, 4, 5, and 7 in the above QC story steps.

In QC results are of course important, but process is even more so. Through the QC story, we can concretely study the methods of reaching the goals and solving problems—Are they analytical? Are they scientific—and evaluate the efforts, thought, enthusiasm, and tenacity of the people involved. Some people rely on their own experience, sixth-sense, and gut feelings. Once in a while they may succeed, but such a success cannot be duplicated, nor can there be prevention of recurrence in case of failure. For that reason, too, QC activities must follow closely the nine steps of the QC story.

As members continue to solve their themes, the methods they have studied before, such as the cause and effect diagram and the Pareto chart, become insufficient. They will want to study more and master the seven tools of QC. They may even choose to study more sophisticated methods and acquire knowledge in physics, chemistry, electronics, and other disciplines that are closely related to their own work.

In QC circle activities the actual experience of solving a problem is very important. People grow through this kind of experience. As they repeat the process of acquiring new knowledge, their abilities expand still further. Their capability grows in such a way that they will be able to solve problems that cannot be solved by college-trained engineers.

V. EVALUATION OF QC CIRCLE ACTIVITIES

Evaluation of QC circle activities must not be confined to study of their results, especially when the end results involve monetary factors. Monetary results must be taken with a grain of salt, because such results can be quite different from one workplace to another. For example, in a workplace that is engaged in mass production, a little effort may result in a saving of millions of dollars. In contrast, in an office that has rationalized its voucher system, the monetary result may be merely a saving of ten thousand dollars or so. In a place that has never had a quality control program, however, once QC circle activities are introduced, millions in savings may result. On the other hand, a steady improvement effort in management that lasts a number of years may not show its results in monetary terms.

Thus evaluation must emphasize factors such as the manner in which QC circle activities are conducted, the attitude and effort shown in problem-solving, and the degree of cooperation existing in a team. Here is one example of the weighted evaluation method:

Selection of the theme	20 points
Cooperative effort	20 points
Understanding of the existing condition and the method of analysis	30 points
Results	10 points
Standardization and prevention of recurrence	10 points
Reflection (rethinking)	10 points
Total	100 points

As illustrated by this example, the results receive only ten points.

VI. QC CIRCLE ACTIVITIES AND SUPERVISORY FUNCTIONS

Here the term "supervisory functions" is used to designate the functions performed by those managers, division heads and section chiefs, engineers, and others who are the superiors of a given quality circle, and those who are colleagues of those superiors. At times I call them members of the PTA for quality circles. Unless PTA members show interest in and support QC circle activities, the latter cannot be nurtured continuously. It is true that QC circle activities are voluntary in nature, but they are conducted within the company. Thus unless the people who exercise supervisory functions support such activities, they cannot succeed.

QC circle activities provide mirror images of top and middle managers in their work. A president who is enthusiastic about QC can count on successful QC circle activities in his company. If a division head for one reason or another shows lack of interest, that division's QC circle activities will suffer.

The following are some dos and don'ts for those who are in supervisory functions:

1. Study quality control and total quality control diligently and show your support. Practice QC with your colleagues who are also in supervisory functions as part of your company's TQC.

2. Give your support to QC circle activities and be prepared to lead them when needed. Your backing must be based on your true understanding of the fundamentals of QC circle activities as well as of actual conditions within your organization. To know QC circle, you must attend QC circle conferences and other related meetings both within and outside your own company. Learn from the activities of other companies.

3. Remember that QC circle activities are voluntary activities. Do not voice your opinion to interfere, and let the activities move at their own pace. Trust the people who are working for you. Proceed with the notion that man is by nature good.

4. QC circle activities are conducted because of respect for humanity. They have as their goals enhancement of people's abilities. This will in turn help the individuals involved, the divisions, and the company. QC circle can never be conducted just for the benefit of the company.

5. As long as there is a workplace, QC circle activities must be continued. They are not a fad for this particular moment.

6. Show your support for QC circles not by words but by action. Help them when they are establishing their goals, when they are setting up their organizational structures (for example, scheduling meetings

for leaders and promoters), when they are making their educational plans; when they are organizing QC seminars or conferences (within their divisions, etc.), and when they are sending people outside the company. Help them to establish concrete plans and help them in their implementation.

7. QC circles must meet at least twice a month, and preferably once a week. A circle that meets only once a month is a sleeping circle. Some of your workers may want to have more frequent meetings. As their supervisor, do not say, "We are too busy now, don't have a meeting this week." The busier the workplace, the more appropriate it is to have a QC circle meeting. That circle must investigate the reasons everyone must work so hard. A fundamental solution is needed.

8. QC circle activities are inseparable from the company's day-to-day work. Some people consider QC circle to be an additional burden. This attitude is of course wrong, and supervisors must find a way to correct it.

9. Do not seek immediate results; study first. Foremen and workers will become better trained through the circle activities, and before long results will become noticeable. As supervisors you must be patient. Take time to nurture circle activities and promote them.

10. As supervisors you have a lot to contribute. You can help the circles get started, you can approve the themes they propose, and you can check their activity plans and reports. You can also help them find a time and place to meet. You can help assemble and prepare data and materials. You can provide overtime pay when needed. And you can help make awards and create channels through which suggestions can really be accepted.

I am sure there are some points I have missed. It may be redundant, but I must repeat that haste makes waste. Take time, and nurture these activities with deliberate speed.

Some Western managers view the growth of QC circle activities with alarm for fear that their own power might be weakened or that their own managerial positions might be eliminated. I hope no one in Japan will think so. If the supervisor is not very capable and does not study, then he can lose his function as the level of QC circle activities improves. When we first began QC circle activities, we often advised the managers, "Leave small details to QC circles. Let them study the problems and find solutions. This will relieve engineers and managers from trivial day-to-day problems of the workplace and free them to do the work for which they are hired. For example, they can spend time establishing policies and goals and attend to the issues of quality assurance. They can deal with the issues of new product development and technology development. They can spend their time confidently looking forward into the future."

VII. WHY DID THE ZERO DEFECT MOVEMENT FAIL IN THE UNITED STATES?

Shortly after QC circle activities began in Japan, the United States started its zero defect (ZD) movement in small groups. The Department of Defense refused to issue procurement orders to companies that did not participate in the ZD movement, so the movement became a well-established one for awhile. However, it has disappeared completely. In its place QC circle activities seem to have taken hold in the United States.

Why did the ZD movement fail? In 1965 I observed the ZD movement in person and felt that it could not succeed. Here I wish to give my analysis to provide lessons for us not to repeat the same mistakes.

1. The ZD movement became a mere movement of will. It emphasized that if everyone did his best there would be no defects.
2. Starting from that assumption, it failed to teach participants the QC method of implementation. It was a movement without tools. It was not scientific.
3. It decreed that good products would ensue if operation standards were closely followed. As I have discussed in this book repeatedly, operation standards are never perfect. What operation standards lack, experience covers. In our QC circles we insist that the circle examine all operation standards, observe how they work, and amend them. The circle follows the new standards, examines them again, and repeats the process of amendment, observance, etc. As this process is repeated there will be improvement in technology itself.
4. In some quarters, the United States has been strongly influenced by the so-called Taylor method. Engineers create work standards and specifications. Workers merely follow. The trouble with this approach is that the workers are regarded as machines. Their humanity is ignored.
5. The word "kickoff" in the ZD movement sounded fine. But wasn't it another term for commanding and forcing the workers to start a campaign for which they had very little enthusiasm?
6. All responsibilities for mistakes and defects were borne by the workers. Normally the share of the blame that workers must bear is

one-fourth or one-fifth, and the remainder is borne by the managers and their staff. In the ZD movement, those mistakes which were not the making of the workers were considered to be theirs. No wonder the movement went astray. Incidentally, Dr. Juran has also been critical of the ZD movement because of its tendency to shift all the blame on the workers although their share of responsibility should never have been more than one-fifth.

7. The movement became just a big show. The Department of Defense decreed that no procurement orders would be issued to nonparticipants in ZD. It encouraged paper compliance.

8. There was no headquarters to promote a nationwide movement. Had there been an organization like the QC Circle Conference to provide opportunities for mutual development, results might have been different.

VIII. QC CIRCLE ACTIVITIES AROUND THE WORLD

QC circle activities began in Japan in April 1962. They are now widely acclaimed in the West and in all other parts of the world.

Initially, I felt that the activities could only succeed in Japan because of the Japanese social, cultural, and religious background. Assuming that QC activities could be extended overseas, I thought that only those nations which share the *kanji* culture could perform them. I thought the activities could succeed only in Taiwan, South Korea, and China. In fact, Taiwan and South Korea introduced QC circle activities over a decade ago, and these countries now have their own national conferences. (The People's Republic of China did not begin these activities until 1978.)

However, as the QC circle activities became known, many countries began to experiment with them. In Southeast Asia, the Philippines, Thailand, Malaysia, and Singapore have them. In the middle of the 1970s, the United States, Brazil, Sweden, Denmark, the Netherlands, and Belgium joined the ranks. Around 1977 and 1978, Mexico and England also began QC activities. There is definitely a QC circle boom, and I frankly do not know how many countries now have them. I was not certain if countries like England, where elitism still rules and trade unions remain strong, could have meaningful QC programs, but I was proven wrong in 1978 when I visited the Jet Engine Division of Rolls Royce and witnessed the success of its QC circle activities.

I do, however, find one factor rather disconcerting in QC circle activities overseas. Unlike those in Japan where people from the same workplace form circles, many overseas circles are formed as teams with members from various workplaces with different people participating. In some instances QC circles consist predominantly of engineers. What will happen to circles with this kind of composition? I fear especially their inability to insist on total participation and on continuity. In some instances QC circles are introduced not for the purpose of total quality control in which quality always comes first but for the purpose of raising the morale of their participants. Since different countries have different social and cultural backgrounds, differing approaches to QC circle activities are of course inevitable. But I am still concerned that some of the best features of our experience in Japan may not be incorporated in such programs.

I still have those reservations expressed above. However, these adaptations prove that QC circle activities can be conducted by all the peoples of the world. They need not be Japanese. Lately, I have begun to feel that "People are people. QC circle activities—which are consistent with human nature—can succeed anywhere in the world as long as their basic principles are kept and implemented, and regardless of race, history, social systems, or political systems."

CHAPTER IX

Quality Control for Subcontracting and Purchasing

Does your company have basic policies toward subcontracting and purchasing?

If control of subcontracting is not progressing smoothly, seventy percent of the responsibility must be borne by the large corporation.

The responsibility for quality assurance rests with the seller-producer.

In principle, purchasing is to be done without inspection.

I. QUALITY CONTROL FOR SUPPLIERS AND PURCHASERS

On the average, Japanese manufacturers spend an equivalent of seventy percent of their manufacturing cost in purchasing raw materials and parts from other companies (hereafter called the suppliers). Therefore, unless the quality, price, quantity, and the time of delivery of these raw materials and parts are right, the purchaser and the assembler can neither manufacture good products nor guarantee quality to their consumers. For the purchasers, the quality control of the suppliers of raw materials and parts is extremely important.

During the 1950s Japanese car manufacturers and electric manufacturers made inferior products that were high in cost and low in quality. One of the reasons for this was the fact that many of the suppliers were small- or medium-sized enterprises that did not have good programs of quality control. Later these manufacturers selected their suppliers carefully, and the suppliers in turn implemented quality control consistently. The genesis of Japanese products' high quality, reliability, and price advantage was in this turn of events.

One of the main factors that has supported the quality of Japanese products is the high level of quality control maintained by the suppliers. They have worked together with the purchasers to make quality possible.

As discussed earlier, some American companies prefer to produce everything they need themselves. This policy may have come from the fact that they either do not or cannot trust their suppliers. For example, the Ford Motor Company has its own steel mill, which has been excess baggage, so to speak. When I visited China in 1978, one factory manager told me, "Our factory is an integrated factory with great potential." Indeed that factory had an excessive amount of stocks, tools, and machines. I was puzzled by the term "great potential." The factory manager was obviously referring to the excess raw materials and the machines which were not utilized. The potential he mentioned was in fact under-utilization. Fearing that the factory would not be able to meet the assigned production volume, the planners had decided to give it excessive capacity. That seemed to be the story behind it.

The advice that I gave to members of China's National Planning Commission and Economic Commission was "I do not want to say that it is bad to have the sixty or so major projects that you are now planning. The projects in themselves are worthy. However, don't you think you must do something first before you undertake these gigantic projects? At the stage where you are now, when you cannot really manage existing factories efficiently, is there any guarantee that you can manage well the new factories that you are planning? Instead of building more, why not engage in QC? If you do, you can utilize the 'potential' capabilities that you possess. Without much further investment you may be able to increase your production by at least fifty percent, and if conditions are favorable, by as much as 100 percent." This advice is not confined to China. Many developing countries are finding that in spite of huge investments they have made in new machinery, the machines cannot be utilized until the countries have the requisite technical background, and will rot away in some warehouse.

The Chinese use the term "integrated factory." It means that the factory does not rely on subcontracting, and no outside supplier will ever be employed. Everything that the factory needs is manufactured by that factory. There seems to be two reasons which have prompted the Chinese to do this. The first is that in China the distribution system is so archaic that it is difficult to obtain cast metal or parts. So the factory prefers to produce them. The second is that in the event of war, China wishes to have an industrial system that can survive without depending on a network of suppliers. In Japan, parts made in one part of the country are sold in another part of the country as a matter of course, and shipped, for example, from Tokyo to Nagoya or from Kyushu to Osaka. Thus if its expressways or railways were bombed, the industrial network would stop functioning. Japan is not a country made for war!

Hence my second piece of advice to members of China's National Planning Commission and Economic Commission: "Maintaining integrated factories will not help efficiency or quality. China is so huge that adoption of the system of national production and marketing as practiced in Japan may not be appropriate. However, in each of the provinces or special cities, for example in the city of Shanghai, special parts manufacturers and cast metal manufacturers should be established. They in turn will serve as suppliers to major industries." Apparently this advice has been accepted. Lately China has been speaking of creating specialized manufacturers and cooperation among different factories.

In the United States, companies also tend to want to manufacture everything on their own. On the average, American manufacturers purchase only about fifty percent of their production cost from outside suppliers. Would it not be better for American manufacturers to purchase about seventy percent of their production cost just as Japanese manufacturers do? It is true that the two countries do not share the same conditions, and generalization can be dangerous. Yet, purchase of a larger proportion of the production cost from specialized manufacturers invariably creates better results in terms of quality, cost, and accumulation of technical know-how. Incidentally, Ford's steel mill is now seeking technical cooperation with a Japanese steel maker.

To return to the main subject, I always tell managers that their long-term basic policy with regard to subcontracting and purchasing must be made very, very clear. The procedure should be:

1. Select a specialized manufacturer. In regard to the parts needed for your company, make it clear which are the ones you want to purchase from this supplier, and which are the ones you want to produce yourself. A clear line of demarcation must be made from the outset.

2. Do you want your subcontractor (supplier) to become a specialized manufacturer who is independent and can supply products to other companies as well, or do you prefer to make the supplier into a subsidiary within your own industrial system *(keiretsu)*. In that case, is your company willing to assume the burden of managing the subsidiary?

From the standpoint of the purchaser, the relationship between the purchaser and supplier must be made crystal clear before any contracting or purchasing can take place. The above two points will help the purchaser in clarifying that relationship. Many, many years ago, I served as a consultant for the Bureau of Materials of the Japanese National Railways. At that time I suggested that the Japanese National Railways purchase all the paint it used from selected outside suppliers. It used only a small portion of paint, which specialized paint-makers could manufacture in Japan more efficiently. On the other hand, making locomotives and rolling stock was the task the National Railways needed to nurture. Therefore, the two types of endeavor should not be viewed as comparable.

II. TEN QC PRINCIPLES FOR VENDEE–VENDOR RELATIONS

To improve quality assurance and to eliminate unsatisfactory conditions existing between the purchaser (vendee) and the supplier (vendor), the following ten principles were set forth. They first came into being in 1960 at a conference of quality control and were revised in 1966. I believe that these principles are still applicable today. When I introduced these principles to my American audience in 1972 they were well received.

Below is the original English text of these ten principles:

Preface: Both vendee and vendor should have mutual confidence, cooperation, and the high resolve of live-and-let-live based on the responsibilities of enterprises for the public. In this spirit, both parties should sincerely practice the following 'Ten Principles.'

Principle 1: Both vendee and vendor are fully responsible for quality control application with mutual understanding and cooperation between their quality control systems.

Principle 2: Both vendee and vendor should be independent of each other and esteem the independence of the other party.

Principle 3: Vendee is responsible to bring clear and adequate information and requirements to the vendor so that the vendor can know precisely what he should manufacture.

Principle 4: Both vendee and vendor, before entering into business transactions, should conclude a rational contract between them in respect to quality, quantity, price, delivery terms, and method of payment.

Principle 5: Vendor is responsible for the assurance of quality that will give satisfaction to vendee, and he is also responsible for submitting necessary and actual data upon the vendee's request.

Request 6: Both vendee and vendor should decide the evaluation method of various items beforehand, which will be admitted as satisfactory to both parties.

Principle 7: Both vendee and vendor should establish in their contract the systems and procedures through which they can reach amicable settlement of disputes whenever any problems occur.

Principle 8: Both vendee and vendor, taking into consideration of the other party's standing, should exchange information necessary to carry out better quality control.

Principle 9: Both vendee and vendor should always perform control business activities sufficiently, such as on ordering, production and inventory planning, clerical work, and systems, so that their relationship is maintained upon an amicable and satisfactory basis.

Principle 10: Both vendee and vendor, when dealing with business transactions, should always take full account of consumer's interests.

III. SPECIFICATIONS FOR RAW MATERIALS AND PARTS

To engage in the business of manufacturing, the purchaser and the supplier must determine specifications for raw materials and parts. Specifications must be determined statistically, after the companies engage in quality analysis and process analysis and consider their economic feasibility. The matter of determining specifications is a specialized field of study in itself, so I shall not dwell on it, but the following points must still be kept in mind:

1. First investigate if there are specifications for raw materials and parts. If none are available, make specifications.
2. If there are existing specifications, analyze them and decide if they are appropriate.
3. Engage in quality analysis and process analysis (including a survey of process capabilities). Study and analyze defective products, products that require reworks, and complaints from consumers. Use the data obtained to revise specifications continually.

As I have discussed again and again in this book, no national standards or company specifications can be perfect. Consumer demand for quality rises continuously. If manufacturers are satisfied with the status quo, they will find one day that their products can no longer satisfy consumers. The purchaser and the supplier must constantly work toward revision and improvement of specifications. Even today, many companies purchase raw materials without making adequate specifications or accept materials that do not meet specifications. I often advise companies that purchase parts, "Select samples of one hundred kinds of parts and measure all of them. Then compare them against blueprints. You will be amused by the results."

IV. DISTINGUISHING COMPANY-MADE PARTS FROM SUPPLIER-MADE PARTS

Making a distinction between company-made and supplier-made parts (or raw materials) is an important function of management. It means to decide whether to produce parts (or raw materials) within the company or to purchase them from suppliers. In making this decision the management must have a long-range view for the welfare of the company and must take the following points into consideration:

1. Are these raw materials and parts very important to the company?
2. Does the company have the technical know-how to produce them within the company? Does the company have process capabilities? Does the management think it necessary to foster such technical know-how within the company? Is building technical know-how feasible with regard to hiring and training personnel and making adequate investments?
3. Are there makers specializing in these raw materials and parts needed by the company? If there are, do they have the requisite process and management capabilities to meet the demands of the company? The company must make a very careful study of this issue before making any decision.
4. If no specialized maker can be found, the question becomes one of the company's willingness to nurture such specialized makers. In the 1950s and 1960s Japanese auto and electric manufacturers had to face many seemingly insurmountable obstacles. They ultimately decided to create and nurture specialized makers, which in turn made it possible for them to attain the positions they enjoy today.
5. Study all of the above factors from the perspectives of cost, quantity, and accumulation of technology.

Normally, these points are studied by the division of production engineering or the division of purchasing. The appropriate division submits a draft plan to the management for the latter's final determination.

V. SELECTING AND NURTURING A SUPPLIER

When procuring materials and parts from outside sources the purchaser must investigate or audit and pass judgment on the supplier's management abilities, especially those relating to quality control.

There are times when the purchaser can select suppliers freely and there are times when that is not possible. Occasions in which the purchaser cannot select freely arise when the purchaser uses its own products, when the suppliers are company subsidiaries, when there is only one source of supply, or when, owing to contractual obligations or governmental regulations, a specified company is designated as the supplier. My own experience suggests that in the long-run the best system is that of free selection, which will help both the purchaser and the supplier. When such a system is not available, often one party becomes a burden to the other.

The purchaser should consider the following before selecting its supplier(s):

1. The supplier knows the management philosophy of the purchaser and continuously and actively maintains contact with the purchaser. It is also cooperative.
2. The supplier has a stable management system that is well-respected by others.
3. The supplier maintains high technical standards and has the capability of dealing with future technological innovations.
4. The supplier can supply precisely those raw materials and parts required by the purchaser, and these meet the latter's quality specifications. The supplier also possesses process capabilities for that purpose or has the ability to enhance such process capabilities.
5. The supplier has the ability to control the amount of production or has the ability to invest in such a way as to insure its ability to meet the amount of production.
6. There is no danger of the supplier breaching corporate secrets.
7. The price is right and the date of delivery is met precisely. In addition, the supplier is easily accessible in terms of transportation and communication.
8. The supplier is sincere in implementing contract provisions.

To ascertain that the above conditions will be met, the purchaser must visit the prospective supplier and investigate the matters listed below, which involve management audits and QC audits. Normally the division of purchasing is given the responsibility of investigation, with the assistance of the divisions of quality control, industrial technology, production engineering, production control, manufacturing, and accounting.

1. The management philosophy of the supplier. The purchaser must study the philosophy held in common by the manager and the staff. In the event that the supplier is a small- or medium-sized enterprise, the purchaser must study the management philosophy of the owner as well as that of his son. Also investigate the manager and staff in terms of personality, knowledge, management ability, and understanding of quality.

2. The concern shown by the supplier for the purchaser.
3. The organizations with which the supplier presently has dealings. If possible, investigate its present purchasers' evaluation of the supplier.
4. The corporate history of the supplier and its latest developments.
5. Types of products maintained by the supplier.
6. Full particulars of the supplier's equipment, processes, and production capabilities.
7. The supplier's quality assurance system and quality control education and implementation programs.
8. The supplier's control of procurement of raw materials and of secondary subcontracting.

After these surveys are completed, the purchaser generally selects two subcontractors, purchasing from both of them. That is, when I say that procurement must be made from two subcontractors, I mean that the purchaser should procure the same materials and parts from both of these companies. There are several reasons to support this practice. One is that in case of fire or natural calamities (typhoons or earthquakes) and man-made calamity (such as strikes), it is not wise to be dependent on just one source of supply.

After these two companies are selected, the purchaser enters into preliminary dealings with each of them. After these prove satisfactory, the purchaser can establish official dealings. In Japan, many large companies have the tendency to purchase parts and raw materials from one company in a very large quantity in an attempt to control it. This move in essence creates a subsidiary dominated by the parent corporation. However, it does not resolve the issue of nurturing specialized companies. It also creates problems in times of recession. Ideally, a subcontractor should be allowed to sell its products to other companies in addition to the main company. One well-known multi-national corporation in the United States insists on not buying more than ten percent of its total purchase from any single source.

In *preliminary dealings,* in principle the purchaser deals with the supplier for a set period of time on a trial basis. This takes place after the selection of the supplier and after a clear contract on the deals has been signed. During this phase of preliminary dealings the purchaser studies the situation and decides whether or not to continue dealing with the same supplier.

Official dealings confirm the fact that the interests of both parties are best served by maintaining the purchasing agreements for a long period of time. The supplier must continuously strive to improve quality, price, and the efficiency of delivery. The purchaser for its part, must provide advice and assistance if needed and requested by the supplier. The purchaser must continue to examine if the supplier is the one with which it can deal in the future with full confidence. For that purpose the purchaser must:

1. Maintain close contact with responsible parties in the supplier company to find out what is going on in the organization at all times and also to establish a relationship of mutual trust.
2. Examine, analyze, and evaluate the records of the purchaser's acceptance of goods, the records of delivery, and the performance records of purchased goods both during use and after they have become finished products.
3. Engage in a QC audit at the supplier's factory, identifying the important quality issues that are of concern to the purchaser and communicating them to the supplier. If necessary, give appropriate advice to the supplier and help the latter solve the existing problems.
4. Establish a system of giving awards to each of the suppliers for implementing quality control. Through this system promote a quality control program in each of them. The purchaser must also give advice and recommendations to the supplier based on the results of its QC audit.

Suspension of trading can also occur between the two parties, even though the norm is to continue dealing with the same parties. When one of the following conditions exists, suspension of trading may occur: when poor-quality and defective parts and materials are regularly supplied and when the amount of such defects does not seem to decrease; when goods are not delivered on time, and delivery methods do not improve; when cost-cutting measures cannot be implemented as planned; and when the management of the supplier becomes so poor that it is in danger of collapse. In terms of control of subcontracting, good suppliers must be nurtured as much as possible by being made into specialized manufacturers. At the same time suppliers that cannot improve must be cut off. Over two decades ago I had the experience of helping a company reduce the number of its subcontractors from about 400 to 100. The entire process took three years to complete.

Nurturing subcontractors is an essential task for the purchaser. In Japan many subcontractors are not strong enough on their own. If they do not know effective management or quality control, the purchaser must provide opportunities to strengthen them in these areas. For example, the purchaser may sponsor seminars on quality control for its subcontractors' managers, engineers, and QC circles. The purchaser can visit suppliers, engage in QC audits and provide guidance. Generally it takes at least three years to make a subcontractor a good one. The management of the purchaser must establish a long-range policy and consider nurturing its subcontractors for the long-range benefit of both parties.

In such an instance, in the interest of independent management, the suppliers must pay the full amount of educational cost incurred. Some suppliers are rather stingy and do not wish to expend the educational cost. If they fail, the responsibility is entirely their own.

One final word of caution. My own experiences have made it clear that "If control of subcontractors does not proceed smoothly, the parent company must bear seventy percent of the responsibility."

VI. QUALITY ASSURANCE OF PURCHASED GOODS

The purchaser cannot guarantee quality to its customers if the raw materials or parts purchased from the supplier are substandard or defective. Especially in Japan, where most of the manufacturers purchase about seventy percent of their manufacturing cost, the importance of this supplier quality cannot be overemphasized. Quality assurance of parts and materials purchased from the suppliers is the key to the manufacturer's own quality assurance. It is also important to the smooth planning of manufacturing operations, to raising productivity, and to planning cost cutting.

Table IX-1 gives a bird's eye view of quality assurance relationships existing between the purchaser and the supplier.

Step 1 shows the least-developed state of quality control. The supplier ships its products as soon as they are manufactured without doing shipping inspection. The purchaser, also without doing inspection at the point of receiving, sends everything to the manufacturing division. The latter has no alternative except to engage in 100% inspection and select only those materials and parts acceptable for manufacturing. In an even worse situation, the manufacturing division may not engage in 100% inspection and may use defective parts in manufacturing. No wonder good products cannot be manufactured.

This procedure is unsatisfactory. Some companies therefore enter Step 2. Step 2 calls for the purchaser to engage in inspection at the point of receiving and send only good materials and parts to the manufacturing division. However, if the purchaser continues this procedure, it would impose a serious cost burden on the purchaser. At

TABLE IX-1

Quality Assurance Relationships between Supplier and Purchaser				
Step	Supplier		Purchaser	
	Manufacturing Division	Inspection Division	Inspection Division	Manufacturing Division
1	—	—	—	100% inspection
2	—	—	100% inspection	
3	—	100% inspection	100% inspection	
4	—	100% inspection	Sampling or checking inspection	
5	100% inspection	Sampling inspection	Sampling or checking inspection	
6	Process control	Sampling inspection	Checking or no inspection	
7	Process control	Checking inspection	Checking or no inspection	
8	Process control	No inspection	No inspection	

the same time there would be no incentive or need for the supplier to engage in quality control. As I stated earlier, "The responsibility for quality assurance rests with the producer," which in this case is the supplier. In principle, 100% inspection must be done by the supplier. If the purchaser engages in 100% inspection then it must ask the supplier to bear the cost.

Thus the supplier must engage in 100% inspection. Yet even if the supplier engages in 100% inspection, if its methods are inadequate its inspection probably cannot be trusted. This forces the purchaser to continue engaging in 100% inspection. This is Step 3. However, when the supplier's inspection can be trusted, the purchaser enters Step 4 and in place of 100% inspection adopts sampling inspection or checking inspection.

Now, if we are to apply the principle that "the responsibility for quality assurance rests with the producer" within the supplier's own company, the full responsibility must be borne by its manufacturing division. It is not rational for its division of inspection to engage in 100% inspection, so the task is to be undertaken by the manufacturing division. This is Step 5. For this purpose everyone in the production sector must have a sense of responsibility, and everyone must work toward quality assurance that can meet the requirements of consumers. In quality assurance, one cannot simply think in terms of passing the inspection or hope that the inspection will not be too strict. As long as that kind of thinking prevails, one cannot move forward to Step 5.

If the people in the manufacturing division become fairly reliable, each of the workers can inspect the goods he has produced on his own and assure their quality. This is the system of self-inspection. When this system is adopted, the worker knows immediately if the product is good or bad and can take immediate corrective action. In this manner, defective products or products requiring reworks can be greatly reduced. In comparison, the conventional approach is quite inadequate, because it lets the division of inspection notify the manufacturing division about the defective products the next day or a few days later. Prompt action is the key to a successful program of quality assurance.

There may be instances in which although the system of 100% inspection is adopted by the manufacturing division, the number of defective products or products requiring reworks does not decrease. In such instances, productivity does not rise and lowering of cost cannot be achieved. This is the reason for entering Step 6, where process control is to be conducted vigorously by the manufacturing division to reduce defective products. If it is found that lack of process capabilities has resulted in defective products, it is necessary to impose 100% inspection. Then the company must engage in process analysis to raise its process capabilities.

Once control and 100% inspection conducted by the manufacturing division become reliable, all that remains for the division of inspection to do is to act as if it were the consumer and engage in sampling inspection. As this progresses further, Step 7 becomes the obvious next step. At this stage the inspection division may check a few selected samples and inspect them from the standpoint of the consumer; quality assurance is adequate and the purchaser can accept these products with or without checking inspection.

Step 8 describes an ideal state in which process analysis has progressed, process capabilities have increased, and reliable process control has been implemented. In such an instance, shipping inspection by the supplier is no longer required. However, people are prone to making mistakes. This idea is not easy to attain.

Japan did not begin to emphasize quality control for suppliers until the latter part of the 1950s, and a solid system of quality control by suppliers did not develop until three, five, or in some instances, ten years later. Patience and a long-range perspective are the keys when the purchaser wishes to obtain quality assurance from his suppliers.

Once the system of quality assurance is well-established, however, both the purchaser and the supplier can reduce drastically the number of personnel needed for the task of inspection. This reduction is accompanied by a rise in productivity, a lowering of cost, and the establishment of a system of reliable quality assurance. Compared to the United States, Japan has more factories that have a well-established system of purchase fully backed by quality assurance. This system has given Japanese factories the competitive edge in quality, productivity, and cost.

VII. CONTROL OF PURCHASED INVENTORY

Where total quality control is well advanced, companies maintain far less purchased inventory. In Japanese companies inventories are small in comparison to their European and American counterparts. To have a large inventory often works against a company. In the West, companies maintain a large inventory because of concern over long-distance transportation, frequent strikes, ineptitude in switching from one process to another, poor quality of products purchased, and lots that may not be acceptable.

As I mentioned earlier, I visited China in 1978 and was surprised to discover that Chinese officials were so proud of their excess inventory, claiming it to represent their potential capabilities. Another thing that came as a surprise was a statement by several important officials of the National Economic Commission that they knew Toyota's *kanban* system. The *kanban* system invented by Toyota allows a company to receive parts "just in time." It was not possible for the Chinese to implement that system at the current stage of their development. I advised them at that time, "If you do not take your quality control seriously and yet try to adopt the *kanban* system, your factory will simply stop operating."

Toyota's *kanban* or just-in-time system was developed over a long period of time by Toyota and its subcontractors. The system became operative through their incessant efforts in management control, particularly in the area of quality control. If the subcontractors could not provide adequate quality assurance, the lots supplied by them would contain many defective parts, and the *kanban* system could not function. If the company forced application of the system, it would simply stop the factory's operation. Looking at it from another perspective, assuming that Toyota had forced implementation of the system without adequate safeguards, it would then be forced to change its production schedule frequently. This would be accompanied by a delay in supplying blueprints for parts and materials. Subcontractors would not be able to keep up with the continuous change, thus missing many delivery dates. In such an instance, the *kanban* system would be self-defeating.

If quality assurance for products purchased is poor, control of inventory cannot be effectively pursued. The goals of purchased inventory control are to purchase good products, to reduce inventory purchased from outside, and to move inventory smoothly without stopping the production process. To attain these goals, the following must be practiced:

1. Both the purchaser and the supplier must conduct solid quality control.
2. Both the purchaser and the supplier must conduct solid quantity control.
3. The purchaser must not change its production schedule too frequently.
4. The orders that the purchaser issues to the supplier must be clear-cut, and specifications, blueprints, and materials that the purchaser gives to the supplier must be handled in such a way as to leave no room for mistakes.
5. After an order is received, the supplier must promptly fill it. The shorter the lead time the more effective it is.
6. The supplier must have a built-in system of adapting to changes in production schedules.

In a nutshell, maintain a good quality control system and management control system. The rest will follow naturally.

CHAPTER X

Quality Control in Marketing: Distribution and Service Industries

Marketing is the entrance and exit of QC.

The marketing division must perform central roles in TQC.

Do not forget that the marketing division represents the company in dealing with customers.

Any marketing division or store that cannot meet the requirements of customers cannot survive.

Is your division or store merely a place to sell products, to shelve products, and watch sales figures?

No marketing is needed if it simply means discounting. Sell products through quality.

Yes, consumer is king. But there are too many kings who are blind.

I. INTRODUCTION

I prefer to use the term "marketing" rather than the term "sales." When the term "sales" is used, people tend to feel that their only obligation is to the bottom line, as is demonstrated by the familiar saying, "All I have to do is to reach our sales goals." In contrast, when we speak of marketing, we instantly think of operating a business establishment for the benefit of customers. It prompts us to go beyond the concept of sales and envision the greater challenges that await the company.

In any event, quality control in sales and marketing includes not just the marketing divisions of manufacturing industries but also those distribution organizations engaged in selling hard merchandise, including trading companies, wholesalers, retailers, supermarkets, department stores, door-to-door sales, and sales through the mail.

The definition can be extended to include tertiary industries or service industries. Under this category, the following may be included: politicians, government bureaus, transportation (railway, bus, air transport, etc.), finance and banking (banks, insurance companies, securities companies, leasing companies, etc.), communications and information industries (telephone and telegraph, broadcasting, advertising, information services, computer service, etc.), energy supply industries (gas, water, sewerage, electricity, etc.), health and welfare industries (hospitals, clinics, maintenance, cleaning, barber shops, etc.), servicing property (car repair and maintenance, guarding private and industrial premises, etc.), leisure industries (hotels, restaurants, movies, golf courses, video arcades, etc.). And the list can go on. All of these industries have one thing in common—they sell "soft" services (although some may also sell hard merchandise).

Governmental bureaus provide services to the people. It would be better if governmental officials were not called officials but public servants. National defense and police are also service industries. In a newspaper interview, Mrs. Haruko Reischauer, wife of a former United States ambassador, once remarked, "The Japanese people do not understand the meaning of the word 'service.' They think service is to receive something for nothing, or to get the thirteenth piece in the baker's dozen. The word literally means to serve someone, and to enter the military is also part of service." That describes well the nature of service.

TQC applies equally to all marketing divisions. Whether one sells hard merchandise or soft merchandise, there is no difference in the TQC applied. In previous chapters, we spoke of the basic values in TQC shared by all types of manufacturing industries and by all types of workers. Here we are merely extending that principle to the service sector.

Generally, people in the service sector or in the marketing and customer service divisions tend to think that quality control belongs to manufacturers and to people who work in the manufacturing divisions. This is a mistaken assumption. As long as a person is selling a piece of merchandise or a service, he must be responsible for its quality. One may buy a particular product from a subcontractor and sell it to someone else, but when a distributor engages in that act, he assumes the responsibility for quality assurance for the merchandise or service sold. Indeed the distributor is the one who must engage in serious quality control. In practical terms, a distributor must establish clear-cut quality standards for all the merchandise purchased from subcontractors and audit the conditions of quality control prevailing among potential subcontractors before choosing the right subcontractors. Once these are selected, the distributor must provide necessary guidance in promoting quality control among these subcontractors, and if necessary, test them and inspect their merchandise upon receipt. It is also the responsibility of the distributor to provide after-service and parts.

Sears, Roebuck and Company, the well-known United States department store, has had quality control specialists since the 1950s. The store has written its own product standards and maintains an efficient product inspection laboratory. It purchases only from those subcontractors who maintain good quality control. More than ninety percent of the products sold are under the Sears own brand name. It maintains a stock of around 200,000 parts in its effort to provide good after-service.

As discussed in Chapter 4, for more than twenty years Japan has been promoting quality assurance with emphasis on its application at the time of new product development. It is clear that the marketing division has an important role to play in planning for new products (point of entrance), before-service, sales, and after-service (point of departure).

In Japan the companies that succeed are the ones which have total quality control that assures participation by their marketing divisions, distribution systems, and subcontractors. This general rule also holds true for manufacturers.

II. PROBLEMS CONNECTED WITH TQC IN MARKETING (DISTRIBUTION AND SERVICE)

In Japan secondary industries are highly competitive internationally because of their high quality and productivity. In contrast, tertiary industries still suffer from low productivity. Both of these facts are well-known. At the same time, we also experience the phenomenon of trade friction, with Western nations blaming Japan for its small amount of imports. One of the main reasons for this trade imbalance is the Western nations' own lack of effort. But their charge that Japan's distribution system is closed to outsiders and is too complex must be taken seriously. It is also true that the distribution system follows the lead given by industrial groups (keiretsu) and displays some of the characteristics of a closely knit family. There are still some feudalistic elements discernible in Japan's distribution system.

In this section, these trade conditions will be discussed from the standpoint of total quality control.

1. As discussed earlier, people often follow the mistaken notion that QC is the responsibility of manufacturers or of the manufacturing division in their own company. A buyer–inspector of a major department store once told me, "Professor, I wish you people would do a better job of educating those manufacturers in QC. Without it, we cannot do our job adequately." He has forgotten that he must be the one to engage in QC audits of prospective subcontractors and select subcontractors through that process. It is also he who must provide guidance in attaining the goals of QC among his subcontractors. He has forgotten that to do a good job in sales, he must first educate his subcontractors to manufacture quality products for ultimate customer satisfaction.

2. There are always people in marketing who tend to be concerned with short-term gains. Some of them are clever but myopic and have a tendency to follow old-style merchant tactics. These people have forgotten the value of implementing the TQC that could let them grow in their business along with their employees. They have also

forgotten the virtue of sharing profits with employees and being concerned with employees' well-being. In so doing they have failed to build long-term trust and profit.

3. Their sales activities are not concerned with customers' interests and are not geared to obtaining customer confidence.

4. They believe that the job of marketing is merely to sell the products that one has purchased or manufactured.

5. They do not feel any responsibility for quality assurance.

6. They do not feel any responsibility for new product development and planning.

7. They lack knowledge of the products they handle.

8. They do not adequately educate their sales personnel. The lack of education is especially evident in QC.

9. In their process control of sales activities, they rely only on their own experience, sixth-sense, and gut feelings. The control is not scientifically based on facts and data. In other words, the circle of PDCA (plan, do, check, action) does not make its round. What dominates their thinking is the old-style approach that the bottom line justifies everything. There is no thought given to the process called sales which requires process analysis and process control. They do not emphasize process and are concerned mainly with appearance and results. Thus they cannot analyze and probe adequately into cause factors especially into true cause factors. They may be able to undertake emergency measures, but not measures to prevent the recurrence of problems. Therefore, there will be no accumulation of marketing technology within the company. When sales are down, discounts have to be given, and when outbid by a competitor, the company does not probe into the cause factors to implement preventive measures for recurrence. Remember our basic principle: "The work must be reported as a QC story."

10. Too frequently, false data are deliberately supplied, or data with unintentional mistakes are used.

11. Data are often not stratified or categorized but bunched together.

12. Then there are additional misunderstandings. QC can be left to a small group of people; Instead of engaging in QC, let us spend more time making sales; I am too busy, how can I be expected to start QC?; My business is with people, and QC does not apply to them; QC means to inflict wounds on myself; If I engage in QC, I am going to expose all the bad points of my company; No thanks, if I start this business of "control," I am going to lose a lot of money (a belief that displays ignorance about the term "control" as used in QC); I do not really know what it means to be good in one's own work or in understanding the quality of people (for example, what quality can one expect in a good salesman?); etc.

III. MARKETING AND NEW PRODUCT DEVELOPMENT

The basis of QC is *market in,* that is to say, to create products that are sought by consumers. The division which has the closest contact with consumers is the marketing division. It is also the division which is best equipped to discern and discover the needs of consumers. This division must catch the trends and discover the needs of consumers ahead of competitors. It must translate the needs into new ideas and then actively participate in planning and developing new products. It is the responsibility of the marketing division to draft a new product plan that is expressed in the language of the consumer. I said earlier that the marketing division is the point of entrance for QC. In a sense everything begins in this division because of its close contact with consumers.

There are many people who still feel that the task of the marketing division is to sell the new products that are made by the divisions of research and development and manufacturing. It is true that the ideas and plans for new products must come from all divisions of the company, but from the perspective of TQC, the one which must shoulder the main burden is the marketing division because it maintains constant contact with consumers. Do not complain that "we cannot sell this because the product is poor." The correct approach is to participate in the development of a new product. It is too late to complain after the product is manufactured. One must change one's own outlook in this regard.

In the definition of TQC, therefore, "marketing must be an integral part of TQC."

IV. MARKETING ACTIVITIES AND QUALITY ASSURANCE

Quality assurance means to be ahead of the consumers to determine their needs, develop new products, have them purchase these products, perform after-service effectively, and let them use the products with satisfaction for five to ten years after purchase. Indeed the role of marketing in quality assurance is very significant. This is the reason I say, "Marketing plays important roles at the entrance and exit of quality control."

In this section, I shall be dealing with the roles of marketing in quality assurance. This subject is divided into three steps: "quality assurance prior to sales," "quality assurance at the time of sales," "quality assurance after sales." I shall now provide points to be considered in each of these three steps.

Quality Assurance Prior to Sales

1. The basis of quality control is *market in*. The company must produce something that the consumer needs and then sell it. To sell merchandise is called *product out*. The company must always produce something that sells well.

2. The marketing division must analyze the needs of consumers (both present and future) and make draft plans for new products. It must ask the following questions: How many requests are there for development of new products? How much information does the company have in regard to market quality?

3. Formulate ideas for new products and participate actively in the planning and development of new products. This is connected with the task of performing quality analysis on consumer requirements.

4. At the time new products are planned and developed, the marketing division must consider the relative importance of these products and their quality. It must also consider building in forward-looking quality and sales points.

5. Determine whether the product planning is adequate.

6. Make suggestions for testing new products and for product research and joint research.

7. Are you practicing "before-service?" Before-service means investigating the use and method of use of a particular product, cooperating with the consumer in selecting a given product, and engaging in joint research (which is especially important in the case of capital goods).

8. The catalogue, instructions for the use of the product, the repair manual, the service manual, and other documents must be completed. Pay attention to the matters relating to quality assurance and the levels of such assurance to be provided. These issues are also related to product liability prevention.

9. Check the adequacy of product liability prevention.

10. Ask yourself this question: "Does the company have a long-term sales promotion plan?"

11. Education of salesmen, service personnel, and distributors prior to the sale of the new product must not be neglected.

12. Have you made visits to interested parties concerning the new product?

13. When purchasing products from an outside source, can you obtain quality products without inspection? How well do you engage in

quality control of this particular subcontractor? How is this manufacturer selected? How good is the manufacturer's quality assurance system? What kind of quality assurance do you have for the original equipment manufacturing devices?

Quality Assurance at the Time of Sale

1. QC education and education concerning the product must be given to all sales personnel in the company and to those who are in its distribution system.
2. Keep in mind that "before-service" must be performed adequately. Find out from the customer what he needs and recommend a particular product which answers his needs. Make this recommendation from the standpoint of the customer. You are the professional with regard to this particular product, knowing more about it than the customer does. Don't let a short-term profit for your company blind you from making the right recommendation.
3. Ask very carefully why the customer wants this product. How does he plan to use it? Remember, the customer is king but the king can be blind!
4. Check the product before you sell and give adequate quality assurance. Try to find any deterioration in quality. Is storage and inventory control adequately conducted?
5. At the time of the customer's acceptance, what is the percent defective? Were any of the following mistakes made: Wrong products sent? Items misdirected? An order not filled?
6. Check whether warnings concerning the use of a particular product are adequately expressed. How long is the period of after-service or of the guarantee?
7. Can the delivery date be met? Is there any possibility of an out-of-stock or delayed delivery situation that could inconvenience the customer? At each step of distribution, aim for ninety to ninety-five percent rate of immediate delivery.
8. Do you handle adequately any of the following: packaging, transport, or installation?

Quality Assurance After Sales

1. Is the control of the initial flow of this new product adequate? What kind of information or feedback do you get?
2. What is the best way of determining the period of warranty, period of assurance, and period of free repair service? It is wrong to make these periods too long, because inequity for the customers can result.
3. Are the instruction booklets and service manuals adequate?

4. Have your people made the periodic rounds (of customers and distributors) without fail?

5. Are the following adequately handled? The after-service system, the service station, visits to users, service personnel (their technological knowledge, numbers, placing, etc.), parts to be supplied, machines and tools used in servicing? Does the system have the ability to perform immediately the service requested? For example, the ratio of instantaneous service to the total number of requests for service must be carefully monitored. Similarly, when parts are required, what is the ratio of those parts made instantly available to the total number of parts requested? And then the question of the efficiency of delivery must also be raised. Incidentally, how effectively is the service system of the company being utilized?

6. Is periodic inspection conducted effectively? Check to see if you are over-inspecting and therefore causing customers extra expense. (For example, is the periodic inspection of automobiles effective?)

7. Is the question of product liability responsibility adequately handled? Is there a necessity for recalling some of the products?

8. Do you know the percentage of nondefective and defective products that are returned? Do you have adequate understanding of the situation? Have you analyzed and probed into the reasons?

9. When customers complain, is that information channelled immediately to the right person in the right division? Study continuously the degree of customer satisfaction.

10. Have you consistently attempted to bring into the open the latent complaints that the customers may have? Once you start QC, hidden complaints become apparent, and the number of complaints will increase substantially.

11. If your company makes use of the information thus obtained and develops new products, your quality assurance system will improve much further. The marketing division performs the function of suppliers. Therefore, you must study the ten QC principles for purchasers and suppliers listed in the preceding chapter. The flowchart following (Diagram X-1) explains the organization of quality assurance activities of the Sales Division of Komatsu Manufacturing Company, Japan's largest maker of construction machines and bulldozers.

V. SELECTING AND NURTURING A DISTRIBUTION SYSTEM

For a marketing division of a manufacturing company, the selection and nurturing of a distribution system is even more important than the selection and nurturing of subcontractors as discussed in

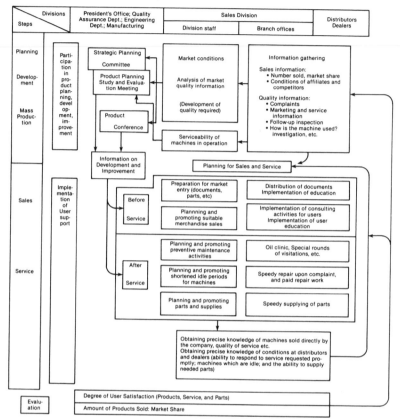

Organization of Quality Assurance Activities, Sales Division
Komatsu Manufacturing

DIAGRAM X-1

Chapter 9. The company must consider this particular task from the standpoint of establishing the company's quality assurance system. There is no one set rule for this process, because selection is influenced by the basic philosophy, policy, and products of a given company. In any event, the company must establish a long-range plan and be concerned with selection, education, and nurturing of its distribution system. Below is a checklist of points to consider.

1. Is it better to have many branch offices and sales offices, or is it better to establish a distribution company? Or is it better to utilize trading companies, agents, or wholesalers?

2. Do you wish to sell the products under your own company's brand name, or under the brand name of the original equipment manufacturer?

3. How do you determine the responsibilities of your branch offices, sales offices, wholesalers, and retailers with regard to sales and quality assurance? Can they handle after-service? Can they accept returned goods and handle complaints? Who will be responsible for the actions taken by those branch offices, etc.?

4. Now check your inventory control system. Who is responsible for the rate of out-of-stock materials and the amount of inventory?

5. You must provide leadership in establishing QC circle activities in your distribution system. You must nurture them. You may wish to introduce joint QC circles between your distributor and your other divisions.

VI. CONTROL OF QUALITY IN MARKETING ACTIVITIES

The basic principles in the control of quality in marketing activities are very simple: educate effectively, clarify objectives, and control the process. QC circle activities can be utilized in this process.

For your reference, certain examples of control items in marketing operations are given below. However, items relating to quality assurance that were given in Section IV above are eliminated from this list.

1. Education and training in TQC and its implementation

2. Promotion of QC circle activities

3. Control of the amount of orders received and the amount of sales (quantity and the amount of money involved)

4. Control of accounts receivable, prevention of bad debts

5. Control of profit

6. Control of inventory: knowing the inventory maintained by the manufacturers, in the distribution system, and in retail stores (amount, assortment of goods, quality deterioration during shelf life, observance of first-in-first-out, products out-of-stock, defective products or parts in stock, rate of inventory control, etc.)

7. Delivery date control (rate of immediate delivery, rate of delivery from subcontractors, etc.)

8. The percentage of hours employees are out of office, the rate of customer visits, the rate of planned visits, and the percentage of hours spent meeting customers, etc.

9. Is there use of pressurized sales tactics? (Maintain a separate card for each retail outlet.)

10. Control of merchandise loss, including loss resulting from shoplifting

11. A company-wide system of quantity control (sales projections and actual performance, inventory in the process of manufacturing, semi-manufacturing and assembling raw materials, and the lead time, etc.)

VII. HOW TO START TQC IN MARKETING DIVISIONS AND DISTRIBUTORS

It has been proven in many companies that QC, TQC, and QC circle activities have had a very significant impact on marketing divisions and on distributors. In spite of this evidence, many people connected with marketing and distributing consider QC to have nothing to do with them, and openly show their disdain. We cannot introduce QC in an atmosphere of misunderstanding and resentment, so we have to proceed carefully before introducing QC.

Generally speaking, the easiest way to start QC in marketing operations is to introduce QC circles, and then move on to QC or TQC. In order to bring QC into practice, I suggest that you start with the solution to some of the division's immediate problems through QC, have your employees experience the value of QC, and then deal step by step with the points listed below. During this period you must concurrently push TQC education among your top managers, middle management, staff members, salesmen, and QC circle leaders.

The list can become endless. The important thing is to begin with problems that are near and of immediate concern to the persons who are asked to solve them. Identify some of the problems which everyone has had difficulty solving. Let your QC circles or people who are performing the same functions get together and solve these problems. In the process, let them realize that QC is really useful to marketing and to distribution. In marketing, even though the location may differ, all sales offices engage in essentially the same task. If you have solved a QC theme do not forget to let the results be known to others. This is a process that I would like to call "lateral dissemination" (applying techniques of successful cases to other areas).

Top managers can begin a TQC program that is clear in its policy goals. Let this top-down TQC join together with the QC circle activities that are characterized by a bottom-up approach. When the bottom-up and top-down processes are successfully incorporated, then your company has the true TQC in which everyone participates.

The task of improving the nature of marketing and distribution never ends. I think the list below attests to that fact.

Points to Consider in Marketing-Related QC

1. Submit ideas for new products answering the needs of consumers. Assist and cooperate in the planning and development of new products. Consumer needs are varied, polarized, and highly sophisticated, so be sure to obtain information concerning the use of these products.

2. Analyze the manner in which you receive your orders, and find out why you sometimes lose to your competitors.

3. How do you make your sales plan? How can you obtain higher accuracy in your sales projections? Analyze your projections and actual accomplishments.

4. Control of the amount of sales.

5. Profit control and expense control.

6. Practice sales promotion and measure its effects.

7. From analyzing the manner in which you receive your orders, move on to the question of how to assemble information concerning orders received. Expand that information, and have a clear understanding of information about the quality needed to meet technical requirements.

8. Lowering the amount of accounts receivable, collection of accounts receivable.

9. Raising the efficiency of work based on estimates, raising the accuracy of the estimates given.

10. Control of returned goods.

11. Inventory control (products and parts), rate of immediate delivery (rate of inventory meeting the exact requirements), rate of delivery from subcontractors, percentage of out-of-stock items, percentage of finished products in the inventory, and percentage of defective goods in the inventory.

12. The manner in which complaints and customer claims are handled.

13. Matters relating to after-service, improvement in the rate of immediate response to service requested, the rate of delivering immediately the parts requested, rationalization of pamphlets and other manuals, improvement in service technology, cost of the product life cycle.

14. Organization and utilization of a list of customers (or clients); rationalization of customer visits, and improvement in the number of

visits to each customer and in the length of time spent meeting customers.

15. Questions related to product liability.
16. Organizing the distribution system.
17. Examination of advertising.
18. Precision, speed, rationalization, and office automation in the sales office and clerical works.
19. Analysis and control of all of the above by stratification.

CHAPTER XI

Quality Control Audit

Do not apply for the Deming Application Prize just for the sake of the prize. Apply for the purpose of promoting your TQC.

Do not promote QC that is perfunctory or merely meant to look good on paper.

Top management often does not know the true state of their company.

When facts are reported, top management must not show anger toward subordinates.

I. WHAT IS THE QUALITY CONTROL AUDIT?

In implementing quality control, one of the most important tasks is to monitor how well it is doing by asking the following questions: Is it conducted well or not? Where are its weaknesses?

The *quality control audit* (hereafter referred to as QC audit) audits the process of quality control implementation, giving an appropriate diagnosis and showing the way to correct its shortcomings. Some people call this procedure by the term *"kansa,"* which is often used in connnection with inspection by law enforcement authorities. Somehow the word reminds me of the philosophical concept that man is by nature evil, and I do not like the term. I use the words "diagnosis" and "advice" instead, believing that all of us must cooperate with one another in order to bring about better conditions for all of us.

The *quality audit* (or quality diagnosis) is similar to the QC audit, but there are differences between the two.

Quality audit means to study the quality of a given product by taking samples from time to time either from within the company or from the market place. It checks the quality of the product to see if the requirements of the consumer are satsified. It corrects defects, if any are discovered, and increases the product's attractive (forward) quality (sales points). In other words, it is an audit that lets the circle of PDCA (plan, do, check, action) turn, instead of merely enhancing "hardware" quality.

In contrast, in QC audits, we examine the manner in which quality control has been undertaken, the way in which the factory builds quality into a given product, control of subcontracting, the manner in which customer complaints are handled, and the methods of implementing quality assurance at each step of production, starting from the stage of new product development. In a nutshell, it is an audit that determines how well the system of quality control functions, enabling the company to take preventive measures against recurrence of bad mistakes. It turns the circle of PDCA on the process of quality control, and becomes an audit of "software" quality. If possible, of course, QC audit and quality audit are to be conducted side by side.

Quality audit shares some similarities with inspection, and QC audit is very much like process control. Conducting quality audit alone cannot insure a long-term practice of quality assurance. In contrast, QC audit is directly connected with judging the quality of products to be manufactured in the future. The basic difference between quality audit and QC audit is in the latter's emphasis on auditing the system and the manner in which the system is operated.

The latest trend in QC auditing is to engage in a total quality control audit (TQC audit) which studies the entire management system. Criteria set for the Deming Application Prize and audits by the president of the company fall within this category. The contents of the audit are also continually expanding.

II. QC AUDIT BY OUTSIDERS

There are four categories of QC audit by outsiders. They are

1. QC audit of the supplier by the purchaser.
2. QC audit conducted for the purpose of certification.
3. QC audit for the Deming Application Prize and Japan Quality Control Medal.
4. QC audit by consultant.

Of the above, number 3 is found only in Japan. The rest is conducted in the West as well.

The checklist for the Deming Application Prize is given below. The prize is awarded case by case, so details differ, but generally speaking, audits are made with this checklist as a guide and effective recommendations are then issued.

A Checklist for the Deming Application Prize

June 17, 1980 Revised

1. *Policy and objectives*
    (1) Policy with regard to management, quality, and quality control
    (2) Methods in determining policy and objectives
    (3) Appropriateness and consistency of the contents of objectives
    (4) Utilization of statistical methods
    (5) Dissemination and permeation of objectives
    (6) Checking objectives and their implementation
    (7) Relationships with long-range and short-range plans

2. *Organization and its operation*
   (1) A clear-cut line of responsibilities
   (2) Appropriateness of delegation of power
   (3) Cooperation between divisions
   (4) Activities of committees
   (5) Utilization of the staff
   (6) Utilization of QC circle (small-group) activities
   (7) Quality control audit

3. *Education and its dissemination*
   (1) Education plan and actual accomplishment
   (2) Consciousness about quality and control, understanding of quality control
   (3) Education concerning statistical concepts and methods, and degree of permeation
   (4) Ability to understand the effects
   (5) Education for subcontractors and outside organizations
   (6) QC circle (small-group) activities
   (7) Suggestion system

4. *Assembling and disseminating information and its utilization*
   (1) Assembling outside information
   (2) Disseminating information between divisions
   (3) Speed in disseminating information (use of computer)
   (4) (Statistical) analysis of information and its utilization

5. *Analysis*
   (1) Selection of important problems and themes
   (2) Appropriateness of the analytical method
   (3) Utilization of statistical methods
   (4) Tying in with own engineering technology
   (5) Quality analysis, process analysis
   (6) Utilization of results of analysis
   (7) Positiveness of suggestions for improvement

6. *Standardization*
   (1) System of standards
   (2) Methods of establishing, revising, and withdrawing standards
   (3) Actual records in establishing, revising, and withdrawing standards
   (4) Contents of standards
   (5) Utilization of statistical methods
   (6) Accumulation of technology
   (7) Utilization of standards

7. *Control*
   (1) Control systems for quality and in related areas such as cost and quantity
   (2) Control points, and control items

(3) Utilization of statistical methods such as the control chart, and general acceptance of the statistical way of thinking

(4) Contributions of QC circle (small-group) activities

(5) Actual conditions of control activities

(6) Actual conditions of control system

8. *Quality assurance*

(1) Procedures for new product development

(2) Quality development (breakdown of quality function) and its analysis, reliability, and design review

(3) Safety and product liability prevention

(4) Process control and improvement

(5) Process capabilities

(6) Measurement and inspection

(7) Control of facilities/equipment, subcontracting, purchasing, services, etc.

(8) Quality assurance system and its audit

(9) Utilization of statistical methods

(10) Evaluation and audit of quality

(11) Practical conditions of quality assurance

9. *Effects*

(1) Measuring effects

(2) Visible effects, such as quality, serviceability, date of delivery, cost, profit, safety, environment, etc.

(3) Invisible effects

(4) Compatibility between prediction of effects and actual records

10. *Future plans*

(1) Understanding of the present condition, and concreteness

(2) Policies adopted to solve shortcomings

(3) Plans of promotion for the future

(4) Relations with the company's long-range plans

QC Audit of the Supplier by the Purchaser

The audits conducted by electric and automobile makers on their subcontractors and by the Defense Agency, the Nippon Telegraph and Telephone Public Corporation (NTT), and the Japan National Railways (JNR) on their suppliers fall within this category.

Problems seldom exist with electric product and automobile makers because they have had extensive experience in promoting their own quality control programs, and they have the knowledge to back it up. When auditors come from these firms, all they have to do is to write good audit reports and recommendations. The subcontractors audited by them will benefit greatly as they plan to promote their own quality control. In fact, it has been through company relationships such as this that Japan's subcontractors have become reliable, specialized makers.

The Defense Agency and the Japan National Railways are not manufacturers, however, and they do not have experience in quality control. Problems can arise rather frequently. In the West the situation is the same. The United States Department of Defense has an impressive manual, *General Quality Control Requirements*, MIL.Q.9858A, but its quality control audit does not function well. Its QC audit often becomes a matter of ineffective paperwork. The audit asks, "Are there specifications and standards to be followed?" "Does the report conform to the formula established?" "Are the data supplied adequate?" What these questions expect are pro forma answers. The audit conducted in this manner ends in judging the results only. It is an inspection not an audit. A QC audit must study the process that has created a particular result, but the pro forma audit overlooks that process. The auditor can have a whole battery of checklists and formulas, but without the knowledge based on experience, he cannot function well.

The QC audit conducted by the purchaser can be a very rewarding experience both for the purchaser and the supplier. If the management of the supplier is merely interested in passing the QC audit, and lets the people responsible for the affected divisions simply produce document after document, it can create only problems. Practices such as this create only "perfunctory quality control," or "quality control for the sake of creating documents." The problem is not confined to Japan but is worldwide. Instead of having an audit consisting of paperwork, why not use the opportunity to subject the entire company to close scrutiny and promote total quality control? The benefits would be much greater than anticipated.

QC Audit Conducted for the Purpose of Certification

The JIS mark and the ASME relating to nuclear energy fall into this category. In QC audits conducted for certification, government officials normally do not have experience in quality control, and their audits, too, may become pro forma. One must guard against that tendency.

Deming Application Prize

The Deming prizes can be divided into two categories, the Deming Prize for individuals who have contributed to Japan's quality control and statistical methods and the Deming Application Prize, which is awarded to industries. The application prize has additional categories in the following areas: Deming Application Prize for Division, Deming Application Prize for Small Enterprise, and Quality Control Award for Factory awarded by the Deming Prize Committee.

The Deming prizes, established in 1951 to commemorate the contributions Dr. W. E. Deming made to Japan's quality control, were funded by the royalties from published transcripts of Dr. Deming's lectures, which he had made available to the Union of Japanese Scientists and Engineers. Over the thirty-year period from 1951 to 1980, seventy-five application prizes were awarded (of which there were twenty prizes for small enterprises). There were also two Deming application prizes for division and seven quality control awards for factory distributed by the prize committee.

To qualify for the Deming Application Prize, the top management of a company must make an application. From the end of July to the end of September, then, a large number of experts in quality control from the Deming Application Prize Subcommittee will be sent to the company to visit each of its plants, branch offices, and the corporate headquarters. These experts, serving as examiners, will audit the current state of the company's total quality control, paying particular attention to its statistical quality control, and will then assign grades. To qualify for one of the prizes, the company as a whole must have scored 70 points or more, the top management must score at least 70 points, and none of the units investigated may score less than 50 points. On passing these tests, the company will receive a medal bearing Dr. Deming's likeness, and a letter of commendation.

This system does not exist in the United States and Europe. At one time, the American Society for Quality Control (ASQC) was interested in establishing a system similar to this and began investigating the possibilities. Nothing came of it, however. Western managers do not appreciate QC audits that are not directly connected with profit, especially when the award consists simply of a medal and a piece of paper.

In Japan, Deming application prizes have been awarded for more than thirty years and have been receiving wider and wider acceptance. Why is this so?

I make a practice of asking the presidents of companies for comments after they receive a Deming prize. One of the most memorable comments came from a person who had been president for over twenty years, and had the reputation of being a one-man-board-of-directors type of person.

"I have been president of this company for over twenty years, yet I had never had the kind of experience that I had while applying for the Deming prize. It was during that time that all of my employees became aware of what I expected of them. They understood the goals I set for the company. They became dedicated workers, and all of them, acting as one body, tried to reach the same goals. Boy, do I love the Deming prize!"

The Deming prizes, established as they were to commemorate the contributions made to Japan's quality control by Dr. W. E. Deming, should not be regarded as mere prizes. I counsel representatives of industries in the following manner:

"Do not apply for the sake of receiving the prize. Application is nothing but the means of promoting total quality control and statistical control in your company. The president must assume the leadership and accept the challenge of a prize audit. His directors, division and section heads, and all employees must follow his lead. Through the application procedure self-rejuvenation of management will occur." By applying for the Deming Application Prize, the company can in the process accomplish true total quality control.

To companies that have applied for the prize, whether or not they pass, "Comments and Recommendations of the Deming Prize Committee" are given. The comments and recommendations contain the findings of the committee about the desirable and undesirable parts of the companies' operations and are accompanied by constructive suggestions.

Japan Quality Control Medal

The Deming Application Prize is awarded annually to a company that has performed well in its company-wide quality control and statistical quality control. Thus there is nothing to prevent the same company from applying again for a second time. Psychologically, however, it can be embarrassing if the company does not pass in its second application. In fact there has not been a single company "courageous" enough to apply for a second prize. Yet even if a company has received the prize once, five years later its directors and middle management will probably be new, and their dedication to company-wide quality control may not be as clear. To answer the needs of these companies, an award that is one step above the Deming Application Prize was created. This came about in 1969 after the International Conference on Quality Control was held in Tokyo. A surplus from the Conference was used in funding a Japan Quality

Control Medal sponsored by the Union of Japanese Scientists and Engineers. Selection of winners is done, however, by the Deming Prize Committee. Only those companies that have received a Deming prize five or more years earlier may apply. Otherwise the criteria for selection are similar to those of the Deming prize, with an additional stipulation that the passing grade is to be 75 and not 70 points.

QC Audit by Consultant

In this system, consultants visit companies and factories, remain there for a few days, and make recommendations and suggestions. This type of audit is also done in Europe and America.

In Japan, this type of audit may be done periodically, or as a preliminary to receiving a Deming prize audit, or as an "aftercare" audit after the Deming Prize has been won.

III. AUDIT FROM WITHIN

There are four types of audits conducted internally. They are:

1. Audit by the president
2. Audit by the head of the unit (by division head, factory manager, branch office manager, etc.)
3. QC audit by the QC staff
4. Mutual QC audit

Audit by the president means that the president himself goes to the factory and to different offices to make his own observations, and uses his own judgment in auditing the results of QC activities.

Audit by the head of the unit means that the head conducts his own QC audit of the workplaces within his own jurisdiction.

A QC audit by the QC staff must have a company director responsible for QC as the leader and have four or five QC staff members constituting an audit group to visit each of the divisions, factories, and branch offices. This approach gives the QC staff a sense of management responsibility and as such is highly desirable.

A mutual audit functions exactly as the words indicate. Separate divisions of the company exchange their audit teams. For example, the one manufacturing process and the process following it may exchange team members to audit each other's QC performances.

To provide a representative example of QC's internal audits, I shall discuss QC audit by the president. This is not being done in the

United States or Europe. Japanese company presidents assume leadership in quality control and study total quality control while presidents in Western countries do not seem to be interested.

In proceeding with a QC audit, the first step is to determine if the audit is to be for the total quality control effort or to be a somewhat limited audit based on guidelines to be issued. In either event, let each of the divisions subject to the presidential audits prepare and submit "an exploratory report on implementation of quality control." The president, accompanied by several of his directors, will then visit factories, offices, and separate divisions of the headquarters and ask each of the units subject to audit to explain the following enumerated items. The explanation must be accompanied by data. After the explanation is over, there should be a period of questions and answers.

The explanation must include the following:

1. Under what policies and objectives, has the unit proceeded with its quality control?
2. What kinds of results have been obtained, and by means of what procedures? (The report must not consist merely of the results. Let the unit show the process through which the results are obtained. Let them report their efforts as QC stories.)
3. What kinds of problems still exist today?
4. Under what policies and objectives, does the unit expect to proceed with quality control in the future?
5. What suggestions does the unit want to give to the president and to the headquarters staff?

Ideally, questions and answers on the above should be traded in the morning when everyone is present. This should be followed by afternoon sessions consisting of visits to workplaces such as the divisions of research and development, manufacturing of prototypes, purchasing, manufacturing, quality control, marketing, and office functions. All the auditors who are taking part in the QC audit are expected to attend these sessions. They are to study all of these units, investigate their QC activities, and participate in separate sessions devoted to questions and answers.

The final session of the presidential audit consists of remarks and suggestions. A presidential audit report may be sent to the unit concerned at a later date. After receiving the presidential suggestions or audit report, each of the units, such as the factory unit, must indicate how it plans to take action and prevent recurrence of mistakes. After each of the units submits its plan, the plan is to be monitored periodically, and a report of complaints with the plan is to be given at the next presidential audit.

The following positive results can ensue from a presidential audit:

1. First of all, such an audit is good for the president. The audit depends on him, so he is forced to study about quality control. He can also observe the actual operations of his factory and other units, which deepens his understanding of his own company. Knowing everything through paperwork is not enough. The president may have an idea of how a particular unit operates and can conceptualize its position in the company, but nothing can supersede actual knowledge obtained through firsthand experience.

2. The president can discover the true state of his company. Normally, truth is not reported to the president. Bad news is suppressed and only good news is reported to him. As I mentioned earlier, if subordinates write candid reports, they can get scolded. So I advise presidents who are about to begin their own presidential audit, "Never get angry when something bad is reported to you. As long as it is true, never lose your temper. Instead, let your employees report on things that are not doing well. Let them give you a candid report of what troubles them. Discuss these problems and try to find solutions together in a spirit of cooperation. After all, the audit by the president is conducted for this very purpose."

3. There will be an improvement in the human relationship between the president and his subordinates. The president is usually so busy that he does not have a chance to meet section chiefs, staff members, and foremen face to face. The audit provides an opportunity to meet, to talk, and to listen. They will develop a feeling for one another and their relations will improve. After the audit, why not have dinner together?

4. For the people whose QC activities are audited, it is also a significant occasion. There are always ups and downs in human activities. There are times when a person can devote full energy to work, and there are times when a person only goes through the motions. The presidential audit is an occasion for challenging employees and stimulating vigorous activities in quality control and total quality control. It also insures continuation of QC circle activities.

It is important to note that the president himself must be the one to conduct the audit. This is especially important in Japan. We all know how busy the president is, but he must make time for the audit. If an Executive Vice-President acts on his behalf, the results would be only one-half as effective.

At first the president may not know how to conduct his audit. To make up for his inexperience, he can have consultants accompany him, and turn to them for necessary assistance. The president should be candid and create a mood that allows free flow of information and discussion.

The above is a mere outline. My suggestion to a company is to proceed with QC audits both from within and without. They can be of immense help to the company.

CHAPTER XII

Utilization
of Statistical Methods

In every work there is dispersion.

Data without dispersion are false data.

Without statistical analysis (quality and process analysis), there can be no effective control.

QC begins with a control chart and ends with a control chart.

Without stratification, there can be no analysis or control.

Ninety-five percent of the problems in a company can be solved by the seven tools of QC.

Statistical methods must become common sense or common knowledge to all engineers and technicians.

I. THREE CATEGORIES ARRANGED ACCORDING TO DIFFICULTY

Statistical methods were used sporadically in Japan before and during the Second World War. It was not until 1949 that they were fully utilized. It was in that year that the Union of Japanese Scientists and Engineers established a Quality Control Research Group and began investigating application of statistical quality control and statistical methods to industries.

I divide statistical methods into the following three categories according to their level of difficulty.

1. Elementary Statistical Method (the so-called Seven Tools)

1. Pareto chart: The principle of vital few, trivial many
2. Cause and effect diagram (This is not precisely a statistical technique)
3. Stratification
4. Check sheet
5. Histogram
6. Scatter diagram (Analysis of correlation through the determination of median; in some instances, use of binomial probability paper)
7. Graph and control chart (Shewhart control chart)

The above are the so-called seven indispensable tools for quality control that are being used by everyone: company presidents, company directors, middle management, foremen, and line workers. These tools are also used in a variety of divisions, not only in the manufacturing division but also in the divisions of planning, design, marketing, purchasing, and technology. From my past experience, as much as ninety-five percent of all problems within a company can be solved by means of these tools. These seven indispensable tools are sometimes likened to the seven tools of Benkei, the twelfth century warrior. Unless a person is trained to use these simple and elementary tools, he cannot expect to master the more difficult methods.

In the case of Japan, the fact that top management down to line workers can use these seven tools is quite significant. In fact, the rate of utilization is perhaps the best in the world. Over 99.9 percent of Japanese people graduate from middle school and anywhere from 92 to 93 percent graduate from high school. They do not find it difficult to use these tools.

Along with these tools, workers must also be trained in the following basic points:

1. The concept of quality—respect for consumers, belief in the fact that the next process is a customer, and a feeling for quality assurance.
2. Principles and implementation concerning management and improvement—control circles, the circle of PDCA, and QC story.
3. A statistical way of thinking—Data have their own distribution and are scattered. Knowing this one must be able to use the data to make a statistical estimate and pass judgment on an action to be taken, or to devise crucial statistical tests, etc.

2. Intermediate Statistical Method

This includes the following:

1. Theory of sampling surveys
2. Statistical sampling inspection
3. Various methods of making statistical estimates and tests
4. Methods of utilizing sensory tests
5. Methods of design of experiments

This method is taught to engineers and members of the QC promotion division. In Japan it has been used effectively.

3. Advanced Statistical Method (using computers concurrently)

This includes the following:

1. Advanced methods of design of experiments.
2. Multivariate analysis.
3. Various methods of operation research (OR).

Only a very limited number of engineers and technicians will be trained in the advanced statistical method in order to be employed in very complicated process analysis and quality analysis. As will be discussed later, this advanced method has become the basis for establishing high technology and also for technology export.

The use of intermediate and advanced statistical methods along with computers, has reached a very high level in Japan. This has also aided in raising the level of Japanese industry.

II. PROBLEMS CONNECTED WITH UTILIZATION OF STATISTICAL METHODS IN INDUSTRIES

More than thirty years have passed since we first began using statistical methods in our industries in 1949. During this period, we have encountered a number of problems. In promoting statistical quality control, we have used the slogan, "Let us talk with data" (let us utilize statistical methods). But despite our efforts we still have many unresolved problems. They are:

1. False data, and data that are not consistent with facts

There are two instances in which data and facts differ. One occurs when the data are artificially created or falsely revised. The second occurs when wrong data are produced because of ignorance of statistical methods.

Why do people deliberately create false data or revise data? This happens more often in companies that are highly centralized and where the top management is accustomed to giving orders. False data are created when people in the top management do not have a sense of dispersion in statistics.

2. Poor methods of collecting data

When I first started my work in quality control, I discovered that data in chemical and metallurgical industries were often distorted. This was due to the fact that the existing sampling method, division method, and measurement and analysis method were inadequate. I wrote a book on statistically sound sampling (*Sampling in Industries*, Tokyo; Maruzen, 1952), and then helped the Union of Japanese Scientists and Engineers establish the Sampling Study Group in Mining Industry. The group was divided into subgroups on iron ore, nonferrous metals, coal, coke, sulfide ore, industrial salt, and sampling instruments. Theories and experiments in sampling, division, and measurement and analysis methods were fully investigated. On the basis of these we established a number of JIS standards. In the case of iron ore, Japan's JIS became the accepted standards for the International Standards

Organization (ISO). Inasmuch as iron ore is traded internationally, setting up the standards for it has also helped smooth the functioning of international trade. In more recent years, Japanese standards on manganese ore and coal have been studied by the ISO for eventual acceptance.

However, many problems remain. Take the issue of environmental protection. When a person attempts to determine a parts per million order, if he is not careful no one will be able to understand what he is doing because of errors in sampling or in measurement and analysis.

Now assuming that the data are given at 56.73 percent, correct interpretation of the data cannot be given unless one knows the margin of error, which can be plus or minus 2%, 0.2%, or 0.02%.

Suppose that there is an odd regulation stating that mercury need not be detected, but that lately measuring instruments have become very sophisticated, and it is possible to obtain numerical values down to the sixth or seventh decimal place. For example, there may be a numerical value of 0.0000005% for mercury. Assuming further that the government requires its detection on this basis, then mercury may be detected everywhere in Japan.

If the accuracy of this sampling or measuring method is plus or minus 0.0002%, and if the numerical value is to be rounded to the fourth decimal place, then 0.0000005% becomes 0.0000%. In that case, does it mean that mercury cannot be detected at all anywhere in Japan?

Thus when there is an error in the data, one cannot determine whether or not the goal of environment protection has really been met. Yet, unfortunately, regulations issued by governmental bureaus often do not take into account errors existing in statistical data.

3. Wrong transcription of data and wrong calculation

Errors arising from elementary mistakes happen to be fairly frequent. Fortunately, those who are experts in statistics can detect them easily.

4. Abnormal value

Data about society in general and about industry are often dirty data, containing abnormal values. In many instances, this has been caused by 1., 2. and 3. above, but data have also been known to contain abnormal values actually in existence. Whether or not to use these data and whether or not to retain the abnormal values are the questions to be determined by considering the purpose that these data are meant to serve and the actions to be taken on the basis of these data.

5. Robustness

Actual data are often not consistent with normal distribution. They also often contain abnormal values. How do they affect statistical methods and the conclusions obtained? Generally advanced tools and sophisticated statistical methods lack robustness—are of limited application, and may not be suitable for use in such cases. However, the seven basic tools described earlier are robust, and can be used in any given situation.

6. Wrong method of application

Those who are inexperienced often make mistakes in using statistical or analytical methods. This is caused by their lack of clear understanding of statistical theories and structural models. My advice is to have seasoned specialists oversee the work of beginners.

III. STATISTICAL ANALYSIS

In industries, statistical methods are most frequently used as tools for analysis. In analysis, there are two major categories. One is quality analysis and the other is process analysis.

Quality analysis is analysis which, with the aid of data and statistical methods, determines the relationship between true quality characteristics and substitute quality characteristics. (See Diagram XII-1.)

Process analysis is analysis which clarifies the relationship between cause factors in the process and effects such as quality, cost, productivity, etc. when one is engaged in process control. Process control attempts to discover cause factors that hinder the smooth functioning of the manufacturing process. It thus endeavors to find technology that can engage in preventive control. Quality, cost, and productivity are effects or results of this process control. (See Diagram XII-2.)

Ninety-five percent of the process analysis can be accomplished through the use of the seven tools. However, in very complicated processes, for example those found in steel mills, advanced techniques are needed. In such cases, the utilization of computers is a must.

One of the strengths of Japanese industry has been its success in dynamic online computer control through the effective handling of

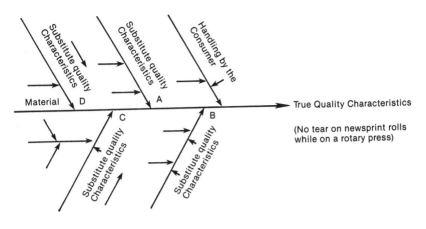

Quality Analysis

DIAGRAM XII-1

process analysis. In fact, we can now boast that the defect rate (fraction defective) is less than one per million (ppm) in our process control. Through the process analysis, we can study statistical process capability.

IV. STATISTICAL CONTROL

In various control measures, such as the circle of PDCA (plan, do, check, action), one recurring problem has been how to check the

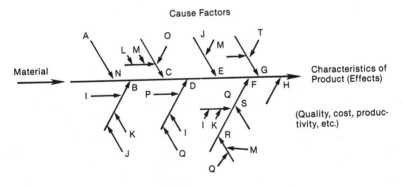

Process Analysis

DIAGRAM XII-2

results. Normally, if things go well, checking is really not necessary. When there are unusual occurrences, however, the law of exception will apply, and all the control measures must be checked to provide bases for judgment.

However, one must remember that causes that can affect the manufacturing process and all other types of work (which constitute a process) are unlimited. Thus the effects (the results of all types of work) will be dispersed. In other words, there will always be a statistical distribution. When we check, therefore, we must be guided by the concept of distribution.

The most convenient tools for this purpose are the three sigma control charts invented by Dr. W. A. Shewhart. Japan imported these shortly after the war and they are now widely used in statistical control.

The control charts frequently used in Japan today are the $\bar{x} - R$ control chart, $\tilde{x} - R$ control chart, x control chart, p control chart, pn control chart, c control chart, and u control chart. Many managers and workers in various workplaces have used these control charts effectively.

Of course, these control charts can still be improved, but the use of these Shewhart charts has nevertheless been very beneficial to Japan.

V. STATISTICAL METHODS AND TECHNOLOGICAL ADVANCE

The use of statistical methods, including the most sophisticated methods, has become deeply rooted in Japan. However, we must not forget the utility of the simple seven tools. Unless a person can master these seven tools, he cannot be expected to use the more sophisticated ones.

Japan's advance in productivity cannot be dissociated from the use of statistical methods. It was through these that the quality level has risen, reliability has risen, and cost has fallen. The key has been the dogged use of process analysis and quality analysis without fanfare for a long period of time. This has brought about improvement in technology. Some contend that engineering technology enhances technology and management technology maintains it. I do not subscribe to that claim. I cannot see any difference between engineering technology and management technology. The so-called control technique is part of proper technique. One must utilize all the technology at his disposal to strive toward advancing quality and efficiency. After the Second World

War, Japan imported many new technologies from the West. Nowadays, Japan can export her technologies to the West as well. This is in large measure a result of the introduction of statistical quality control and the use of statistical analysis, process analysis, and quality analysis.

Over twenty years ago I wrote "We seek the following for our new quality control movement: We hope to produce good and inexpensive products in large quantity for export purposes, and through this achievement to solidify the foundation of Japanese economy, establish Japan's industrial technology, and create opportunities for exporting technology. Once our national economy is on a solid foundation, we can expect our private companies to divide their wealth three ways, among the consumers, workers, and investors. For the nation as a whole, we seek continuous advancement in our standard of living." Little by little, these goals are being realized.

Of course, many problems still remain, and there is always room for improvement, especially in regard to the use of statistical methods.

If statistical methods can find their way into areas other than industries, perhaps the nation as a whole will become better.

Index